INDIA'S POPULAR CULTURE

iconic spaces and fluid images

INDIA'S POPULAR CULTURE
iconic spaces and fluid images

edited by Jyotindra Jain

Marg publications

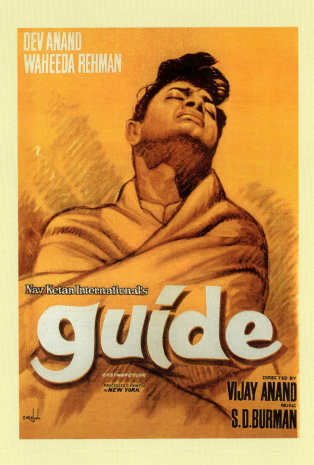

General Editor   PRATAPADITYA PAL
Associate Editor   RASHMI PODDAR

Executive Editors   SAVITA CHANDIRAMANI
                        GAYATRI W. UGRA
Text Editor   RIVKA ISRAEL
Editorial Executive   ARNAVAZ K. BHANSALI

Designer   NAJU HIRANI

Senior Production Executive   GAUTAM V. JADHAV
Production Executive   VIDYADHAR R. SAWANT

Vol. 59 No. 2
December 2007
Price: Rs 2500.00 / US$ 65.00
ISBN 10: 81-85026-81-5
ISBN 13: 978-81-85026-81-7
Library of Congress Catalog Card Number: 2007-340004

Published by Radhika Sabavala for Marg Publications on behalf of the National
Centre for the Performing Arts at 24, Homi Mody Street, Mumbai 400 001.

Colour and black and white processing by Reproscan, Mumbai 400 013.
Printed at Thomson Press, Navi Mumbai 400 708, India.

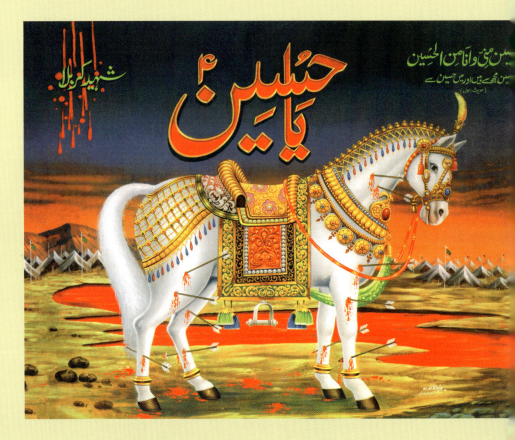

Marg's quarterly publications receive support from the Sir Dorabji Tata Trust – Endowment Fund.

CONTENTS

INTRODUCTION
image mobility
in India's popular culture

Jyotindra Jain

1. Portrait of a lady. Photographer unknown, early 20th century. Photographic collage with painted backdrop, table, and carpet. Collection of Siddharth Tagore, Delhi. The diminutive portrait amidst elaborate colonial paraphernalia is an obvious attempt at iconizing the sitter.

Both "popular" and "visual" as specific forms of modern culture have only recently received serious academic attention in India. Some of the factors which have supplied new frames to these cultural categories are, broadly, the onset of colonialism and industrialized mass-production catering to the new urban middle class; the emergence of modern communication technologies – digital media, TV, and film – and the consequent theoretical developments in the studies of visuality and semiotics; the "visual construction of the social";[1] and anxieties in academia about the definition and scope of the well-established disciplines of aesthetics and art history as well as emergent new disciplines such as cultural studies, film, and media studies.

What is popular culture? Often unreflectively seen as situated solely in mass-production and mass-consumption, it is usually linked to the common culture of the street as against "classical" or "traditional" cultures, to subaltern or working-class culture vis-a-vis that of the dominant groups. Although it is entangled in the histories of such oversimplified binaries as "high" and "low", "autonomous" and "instrumental", "individual" and "communal", "authentic" and "commodified", it has increasingly become possible to critically analyse its locus and role even though these may be continuously shifting with developments in technology, production, the market, and their cumulative impact on culture and society.

Though these quantitative and ideological criteria may serve as broad analytical tools to understand the constitution, role, and location of the popular, the shift in focus from production to reception is the decisive factor in analysing where meaning occurs in the signs of resistance, religious contestation, seizure, and appropriation.

Questions may arise of how commodity images of mass culture can be understood as new objects of art history, and whether this confirms the notion of "visual culture" as opposed to just art history. In a way, the answers are contained within the questions. W.J.T. Mitchell[2] draws our attention to the common fallacy that visual culture tends to wipe out the distinction between artistic and non-artistic images, thereby dissolving the disciplines of art history and history of images. Both "artistic" and "non-artistic" images are a part of the wider "domain of images" and the boundaries between the two cannot be predetermined outside the context of use of an image; they "become clear when one looks at both sides of this ever-shifting border and traces the transactions and translations between them".[3] It is well known that the artistic avant-garde has regularly been propelled into modernity by the objects and images stemming from the commercial culture of the marginalized, with whose struggle avant-garde practitioners had always felt empathy. More obvious examples of this process would be the works of Robert Rauschenberg and Andy Warhol in the West or those of Bhupen Khakar, Atul Dodiya, or Subodh Gupta in India. What about the value of visual culture outside the space of "art"? Well, hasn't there been "a history of the image before the era of art"?[4] Moreover "the founding moments for ... discourses on both modernist art and mass culture were one and the same ... the theory of one was the theory of the other".[5]

The new image mobilization in India – resulting from and feeding into historical and resurgent cultural, religious, and regional nationalism, the rise of political reconfigurations emerging from changing ideological equations, as well as the phenomenon of globalization, consumerism, and diaspora – plays a critical role in the overall organization of social relations and cultural spaces. In this circuit of production and reception of popular Indian imagery, the present volume focuses on issues of purposed photography and the expanded world of the visual image, exploring such areas as concepts of tradition and modernity, the construction of cultural identities, and strategies of representation.

The explosion of the visual as perceived all around us – on billboards, calendars, posters, religious paraphernalia, print-media, and television, in restaurants and shops, on the roadside, in autorickshaws, taxis, trucks, and buses, in bazaars and around temples – emanates from the forces of urbanization of our culture in terms of technologies of image production and ways of thinking and looking. Colonial ideals of perspective and realism in pictorial representation endowed the idealized, traditional imagery with a more tangible and sensual presence. Mass production and circulation of this imagery became a potent instrument in negotiating interstices between the sacred, the erotic, the political, and the modern.

Methodologically, most of the contributors to this volume move fluidly between anthropology, performance studies, art history, and cultural studies within the broader frame of the new discipline of visual studies which is an interdisciplinary mode of studying culture across established mediums and disciplines foregrounding critical estimation of visual images. After a brief summary of the articles, I shall review each author's approach to the notion of the iconization of space through the intervention of the visual image.

Aspects of popular visual culture

Theorizing the issue of modern science and ideology while recognizing that both are different enterprises, Clifford Geertz stressed the point that they are not unrelated; that is to say ideologies indeed make empirical claims and the differences between the two "are to be sought in the sorts of symbolic strategy"[6] that the two sides adopt. Building on this idea of societies giving fresh meaning to traditional cultural features not only to preserve them but to cope with "modernity" through "symbolic strategies", Christophe Jaffrelot, the renowned scholar of the Hindu nationalist movement in India, analysed the case of early Hindu nationalist policy. Hindu reformists of the 19th and early 20th centuries adopted the strategy of an "ideological reinterpretation of the past, perfectly fashioned in order to meet the challenges of the West"[7] by inventing and reinventing past golden ages.

Sumathi Ramaswamy in her essay "Of Gods and Globes" explores the Hindu endeavour of facilitating

2. Varaha avatar. Bilaspur, Punjab Hills, 1730. Opaque watercolour and gold on paper; 21.3 x 15.7 cm. Reproduced with permission from Brooklyn Museum, New York, 41.1026.

the transformation of deities into the modern by infusing scientific cartography into the iconographic conception of the gods. With this theoretical framework, Ramaswamy examines the visual history of Varaha, the boar incarnation of Vishnu, who in the popular culture of the 19th and 20th centuries was depicted in his modern iconographic avatar carrying Prithvi or Earth in the form of a globe. Thus, she brilliantly infers the transformation of Hindu gods into *Indian* gods – "the geo body of India nationalizing their divine bodies", thereby appropriating modern cartographic knowledge to Hinduism.

Indian popular visual culture is often treated as a generalized and undifferentiated category assuming mass-produced images to be "popular" in a quantitative sense. It has been explored in relation to its engendering of nationalist strategies, religious mobility, its role in the study of difference of gender, race, religion, and power, its function in the construction of the social. Christopher Pinney's rigorous follow-up on trajectories of iconic Indian images (for example his work on Bhagat Singh[8]) opens up a larger set of issues, which he explores in his article "The Accidental Ramdev" in this volume. Here he follows up "Ramdevji's mechanically reproduced afterlife" through an image journey, which brings into focus some important inferences for the study of Indian popular culture.

Pinney, with the examples of Ramdevji's chromolithographic image histories, brings to notice how the random combination of facts, such as the role played by a publisher (Harnarayan and Sons, Jodhpur) or patronage of a ruling family (in this case of Bikaner) helped to consolidate his chromolithographic fame. Pinney also draws our attention to the fact that the full-frontal darshanic idiom of the "dominant" class of Vaishnavas as visible in the post-absorptive (wherein the gazes of the character are not absorbed within the picture but are addressed to the onlooker) paradigm of Nathdvara Shrinathji images may be different from the *katha* or narrative aesthetic of Ramdevji images in the chromolithographs where "for Dalit and other followers of Ramdevji, he remains a figure of action, whose profile directs attention to his *jivanlila* [life history]."

Michel Foucault[9] spoke of real places – that actually exist – as against utopias or sites disconnected from any real place. Hierarchical spatial binaries such as sacred and profane places, protected and open or urban and rural, especially of the Middle Ages, were his examples of real spaces that concern real life. Yet importantly, he also spoke of other "real spaces", in which "all the other sites that can be found within the culture, are simultaneously represented, contested, and inverted".[10] He termed these sites heterotopia, which embody the "simultaneously mythic and real contestation of the space in which we live".[11] The spaces of theatre and cinema constitute apt examples for evoking and juxtaposing a number of spaces in a single real place: "Thus it is that the theatre brings onto the rectangle of the stage, one after the other, a whole series of places that are foreign to one another;...."[12]

On account of a definite intervisuality that links the printed image with theatre and performativity besides other forms of visual culture, this volume, though primarily focused on the printed image has an article on painted theatre curtains, and one on the

3. Inlay card of the music CD of songs from *Jai Baba Ramdev*.

4. A still from the play *Maha Bhagavata*, staged by Surabhi Theatre. Krishna giving a sermon. Photograph courtesy P. Sripathi, Hyderabad.

cultural tableaux of the Indian Republic Day Parade. The eclecticism of the drop scene curtains of the Surabhi Theatre, as pointed out by Anuradha Kapur, assumes a lot of traffic between the images from diverse pictorial sources from the 19th and early 20th centuries. The cultural tableaux and folk dances staged in the Republic Day Parade are no less shaped by the print and electronic media, philately, tourism advertisements, maps, and photography.

In her article "Optics for the Stage", Anuradha Kapur examines the painted scenic backdrops of the Surabhi Theatre Company of Andhra Pradesh in terms of the "surplus of illusion", "floating" spaces, and "space of fantasy" evoked by them, and "by which the Surabhi stage appears to accommodate", as it were, "several different spaces within it". Kapur traces the genealogy of the Surabhi Theatre's mise en scene from the plunging curtains that became a crowd puller in 18th- and 19th-century England, and the moulded and gilded border fixed around the Haymarket arch in 1880 which virtually turned the stage into a picture, to the eclectic stage of Parsi Theatre with its enchanting backdrops using the newly introduced devices of geometric perspective that tricked the eye with their painted vanishing points engendering the illusion of reality, and the "seductions of the curtains and the voluptuousness of that stage". The Parsi Theatre, of which Surabhi is a sub-genre, was influenced by colonial India's modern popular imagery that emanated from the pedagogy of the colonial art school that put value on perspective, and from the arrival of the techniques of engraving, lithography, and oleography leading to mass-production and circulation of illusionistic pictures.

My essay on "India's Republic Day Parade" examines this annual Parade to show how the cultural mechanism of image mobilization – of symbols, icons, performances, and spectacles – has been deployed by the state to

5. A still from the play *Maha Bhagavata*, staged by Surabhi Theatre. Yashoda, suspecting that Krishna has eaten clay, asks him to open his mouth. Photograph courtesy P. Sripathi, Hyderabad.

6. Tableau representing
Nagaland, focusing
on a Naga folk dance,
Republic Day Parade, 2006.
Photograph: Photo Division,
D.P.R., Ministry of Defence,
Government of India.

gain ideological control and to strategically ensure the integration of the diverse and separatist elements active in India before and after Independence. Almost throughout 1952, Prime Minister Jawaharlal Nehru (who was concerned about this integration of post-Independence India with voices of dissent emerging from culturally diverse regions) engaged himself in giving shape to the cultural pageant, comprising tableaux of folk and tribal life and dance forms, to be inculcated into the Parade. These tableaux and dances were strategically restored for the purpose of representing the nation's unity in diversity. "Culture" emerged as effect and though its immediate site of production was the Parade, it eventually began to "heal into its presumptive past and its present cultural context like well-set bone. ...judgements about authenticity hard to make."[13]

The visual archives of the Republic Day Parades not only fed their own growth over 55 years but significantly began to provide the standard for authentic cultural behaviour, self/image formation, and construction of identity back in the village and tribal communities. Imitation of the restored image of the self as constructed and projected by the nation began to become the self in the tribe and the village.

Despite the fact that a substantial body of work on Indian popular culture has emerged in the recent past influencing deliberations on Indian history, sociology, and art history, for some curious reasons the Islamic popular culture of India/South Asia has received little scholarly attention. While the area between iconoclasm and idolatry, discourse and practice in Islam continues to be grey, there seems to be an increasing consumption of Islamic popular visual culture in South Asia. Yousuf Saeed's scrutiny of the region's Islamic calendar art and his fieldwork conducted at important sites in India and Pakistan has led him to achieve some revealing insights into this lesser known area of study.

The eclectic character of Islamic printed images results from the collage-like assimilation of several diverse elements, where an arch or a dome may come from old photographs of Mecca and Medina, a saint's person may be derived from an old painting, the

landscape from Swiss calendar pictures, and *diya*s or lamps from a Hindu poster. These images interpret the icons of the local shrines in relation to the images of Mecca and Medina.

As proposed by Arjun Appadurai, the social meaning and value of a cultural object may be located in its human transactions, through its historical circulation by following its forms, contexts of uses, and its trajectories – "it is the things-in-motion that illuminate the human and social context".[14] In this processual approach, the emphasis is placed on mobility and migration, life histories and trajectories of things with an accent on temporality, while the possibility of concurrent spatial diffusion is not overlooked.

Ranjani Mazumdar in her article "The Bombay Film Poster" traces the historical development of the film poster in terms of its formal aesthetic transformation, its cultural biographical mobility, and its spatial diffusion. Using the developments in modern technologies – from oil painting, photography, lithography, and offset printing, to computer generated imagery – as a starting point, Mazumdar illuminates how the need for gloss

7. Stereotyped images of members of the Muslim community could have been inspired by scenes from Hindi feature films produced in Mumbai, especially depicting the "Muslim Social" – a genre that became popular in the 1960s and '70s. Artist unknown, Publisher: J.B. Khanna & Co.

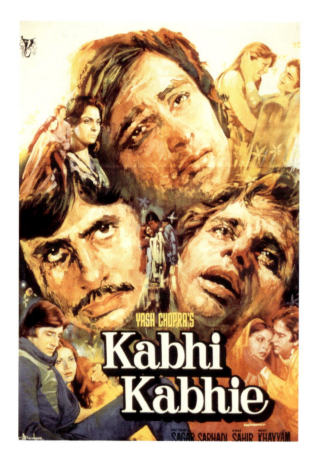

British Indian photography (which itself was not syncretic) with that of its Portuguese Goan counterpart as both have divergent social histories. The Goan photographic archive centred around family portraits of two elite classes – the feudal landed class thriving on the traditional rice and coconut crop, and the Western-educated elite which had evolved a style of dressing and social etiquette based on the role model of the local European population. This convention played a crucial role in constructing Goan identity that was to percolate down to every stratum of Goan society – "the photographic representation is clearly addressed to indigenous social hierarchies".

One specific characteristic of Goan family photographs observed by Viegas is that photography gave a new visibility to conjugal and extended family values that were further legitimized by such visual symbolic markers as the church and the family house. The values and challenges of the Victorian era arrived in the colonies where the native population absorbed

8. Poster for *Kabhi Kabhie* directed by Yash Chopra (1976). Photograph courtesy National Film Archive of India, Pune.

and luminosity brought the poster close to electronic media images and cinema itself. The poster compacts and condenses the film it represents as hierarchized information presented in the order: star/story/title and credits. In doing this, the poster juxtaposes different images wherein those of the stars are shown more prominently than other characters or the details of the locations (house, street, landscape, etc.).

Mazumdar traces the many lives of the Indian film poster as it "moves from *dhaba*s and city walls to lavatories, from *pan* shops to huts". Interestingly, as it moves from the street into the enclosed space of a hut, a shop, or a gallery, the poster begins to acquire an aura – a sort of "museum effect".

Like "oriental", the term "colonial" has long been used quite indiscriminately. In the case of India, Portuguese, French, or British colonial cultural traits have often been considered under one general category of "colonial Indian" connoting "European", "British", "Western", or simply "modern". Savia Viegas in her article "The Family Archive" draws attention to a possible trap in equating the specificities of colonial

9. Posing against a forest backdrop, 1940. Photograph: Lord's Studio, Margao.

them as markers of the progressive era, reinventing themselves in the upper rungs of the social hierarchy through the power of photography.

As pointed out by Noam Chomsky, new forms of global capitalism seem to be "going in opposite directions."[15] On the one hand, there is a distinct bent toward "international centralization of power",[16] and on the other, there is an increasing tendency towards regionalism and local autonomy. In terms of globalism's cultural localization this would stand for a paradoxical interface of rising global cultural formations with equally strong local concerns for tradition, nation, and cultural identity. This seemingly paradoxical and polarized space now appears to be giving way to a new local space, which is increasingly globalized, and "binding together the global and the local, the city and the country, the centre and the periphery, in new and quite unfamiliar ways".[17]

Christiane Brosius in her article "The Enclaved Gaze" probes this new and unfamiliar global Indian lifestyle where apparent paradoxes such as tradition and modernity, history and the present, amalgamate "harmoniously". Hinging her study upon the visual and textual material of lifestyle advertisement, Brosius explores the new Indian middle class's lifestyle space in which generalized history, tradition, and modernity interlock with nostalgia, exoticism, and desire. Brosius points out that "'history' gives depth and feeling to nationality and cosmopolitanism", and hence great fascination lies with historical architecture and ancient sites as well as with the exotic images from souvenir cultures spanning the globe, which is emphasized in such promotional lifestyle advertisements as, for example: "The place where Egyptian Grandeur mingles with ultra-modern lifestyle", "Seek out a kingdom worthy of thyself", "Parthenon-like balconies".

Image mobility and the iconization of space

The double focus of the essays in this volume is set on the complex course of visual image production in the modern era and its migration through highly layered spaces; in this very process, these spaces are reinvented through symbolic gestures and ritualization, thus reconstructing them as anchored or portable, "pure" or heterogeneous, reductive or expansionary, for strategic objectives.

10. Brochure for Omaxe township in Gurgaon, 2005.

As mentioned earlier, Ramdevji's depiction, largely in profile, which Christopher Pinney relates to the *katha* (narrative) aesthetic in contrast to the darshanic (frontal) aesthetic typical of the Shrinathji images of the upper-class Vaishnavas, plays a crucial role in defining the ritual spaces of the dominant class as against those of the marginalized (Dalit and other followers of Ramdevji). The full-frontal idiom mobilized the spaces created by theatre and cinema, which got smoothly absorbed in the dominant-class aesthetic of the Vaishnavas. Alternatively to Pinney's ritual activation of real geographic spaces as well as evocation of those of dominant and marginalized classes through the intervention of cultic pictures, Anuradha Kapur explores the mobilization of "floating spaces" engendered by the painted backdrops of Surabhi Theatre performances for the effect of "surplus of illusion" and creation of a "space of fantasy" and several other spaces which are simultaneously set in motion in different time zones.

Yet another image-space correlate is investigated by Brosius who connects the visuals of the opulent new lifestyle advertisements with the dream world of modern living of the recently emerged wealthy Indian middle-class. Here the heterogeneous spaces of the modern Indian lifestyle emerging from the new globalized economy and comprising an eclectic assemblage of traditional Indian architectural features, which evoke the spaces of India's past golden ages and thereby of the nation itself, go hand-in-hand with equally random accumulations of cosmopolitan and international trends in a composite space of fantasy, desire, global modernity, history, tradition, and nation rolled into one in search of a new democracy of consumption.

Nations are in the habit of mobilizing visual symbols, performances, and spectacles to establish an identity and sustain their integrity. Though they dig, discover, and harness tradition and history in the process of nation-building, they leave a window open for new possibilities to appropriate modernity by reinterpreting its elements to strengthen its particular objective and self/image. The role of India's Republic Day Parade (Jyotindra Jain) and that of the transformation of the Varaha image as it occurs in Indian popular culture

in consolidating the nation (Sumathi Ramaswamy) provide two more examples of the notion of iconization of spaces.

India's post-Independence cataloguing of visual symbols such as the national flower, the national bird, and the national animal (some of which are constituents of the Bharat Mata, Mother India, image) and the systematic structuring of the Republic Day Parade, the pageant and performances comprising cultural tableaux depicting highly romanticized versions of landmarks in Indian history, essentialized representations of tribal and village communities, traditional handicrafts, etc. (culture's modern face is hardly represented here but modern weaponry and symbols of modern technological and economic progress are valorized) exemplify how the space of the Indian nation is strategically consecrated in the service of the unity-in-diversity image of the country. By deliberately selecting certain historical events for representation in the pageant and by tactically putting frames of the imaginary Indian tradition around cultural performances, an abstract, generalized space of the Indian nation is thus dreamed up.

Replacing Prithvi (traditionally depicted as a young maiden) by a globe (both as symbol of modern knowledge and a "shrine" to Bharat Mata) in the iconography of Varaha in Indian popular images represents not only an act of centralizing the space of the Indian nation within the globe but one of anointing the space as "Hindu" through the mobility of images of Hindu gods.

In Nehru's ideology of "unity in diversity" it was the "unity" of the nation which was the desired objective to be effected through the amalgamation of its diverse regional cultural zones and was therefore prioritized over "diversity". However the regions themselves through their particular social and cultural histories, including the colonial and post-colonial ones, had constructed spaces articulating their own regional identities. The colonial state too contributed in shaping these identities through their enlightenment projects and mechanisms of governance such as the anthropological and linguistic surveys, the census and the map.[18] Besides ethnicity, religion, and citizenship, a major marker of cultivating such identities was regional visual culture.

Images from the archives of Goan family photographs (Savia Viegas) and those from popular Indian Muslim religious art (Yousuf Saeed) follow their own concentric logic which questions the easy binaries such as inside vs outside, believer vs non-believer, canonical vs vernacular, etc. Both Viegas and Saeed emphasize the processes of the regional construction of the social. Viegas follows the trajectory of Goan social history through photography, in the background of specific Portuguese colonial cultural values and economic policies as well as indigenous social hierarchies leading to a representation which "borrows some of the power and currency embedded in the [Victorian] setting while remaining rooted in its own social milieu".

Although canonical Islam considers idolatry un-Islamic, there has been a massive growth of Islamic popular culture in the form of calendar prints and cultic souvenirs, which is absorbed into the living religious practices of regional forms of Islam such as in India. As in the case of Goan photography, there, too, the indigenous social milieu begets distinctly local forms of popular culture, which collapse the dichotomy of canonical and vernacular, subverting hegemonic claims to a pan-national, monolithic Islam.

Ravi Varma's technique of assimilating "quotes" from heterogeneous visual sources on a single canvas engendered ambivalent spaces, which evoked mixed cultural responses. This collage effect led to the emergence of multiple perspectives in his paintings due to a lack of the requisite foreshortening (which automatically happens in naturalistic painting), generating fantastic spaces. Ravi Varma's pictures are clearly informed by the visual contexts of the theatre and photography of his time where painted backdrops were used, and the lack of the requisite foreshortening of figures vis-à-vis the backdrop has caused the figures to appear as cutouts or tableaux. This effect of temporal and spatial diffusion is dealt with by Ranjani Mazumdar (and differently by Anuradha Kapur). Mazumdar traces the genealogy of the Bombay film poster in

its historical aspect and its formal and conceptual construction considering the various factors that cause a hierarchization of images on its surface.

As the hierarchy-driven conceptual juxtaposition of images on the surface of the poster collapses all rules of geometric perspective, it opens up a possibility for the images to float in the space and time of fantasy – also a dominant theme of Bombay cinema.

NOTES

[1] W.J.T. Mitchell, "Showing Seeing: A Critique of Visual Culture", in Nicholas Mirzoeff (ed.), *The Visual Culture Reader*, New York, 2002, pp. 88, 92.

[2] Ibid.

[3] Ibid., p. 93.

[4] See Hans Belting, *Likeness and Presence. A History of the Image before the Era of Art*, Chicago/London, 1994.

[5] Thomas Crow, *Modern Art in the Common Culture*, New Haven/London, 1996, pp. 36–37.

[6] Clifford Geertz, *The Interpretation of Cultures*, New York, 1973, p. 230.

[7] Christophe Jaffrelot, *The Hindu Nationalist Movement in India*, New York, 1966, p. 13.

[8] See Christopher Pinney, *Photos of the Gods*, New Delhi, 2004, Chapter 6.

[9] Michel Foucault, "Of Other Spaces", in *Diacritics*, 16: 1 (Spring 1986), pp. 22–27.

[10] Ibid., p. 24.

[11] Ibid.

[12] Ibid., p. 25.

[13] Richard Schechner, *Performative Circumstances: From the Avant Garde to Ramlila*, Calcutta, 1983, p. 184.

[14] Arjun Appadurai, *The Social Life of Things*, Cambridge, 1986, p. 5.

[15] Noam Chomsky, *Spin* interview (1003) with Jerry Brown, quoted in Rob Wilson and Wimal Dissanayake (eds.), *Global/Local*, Durham, London, 1996, p. 1.

[16] Ibid.

[17] David Harvey, quoted in Wilson and Dissanayake, p. 3.

[18] For the impact of map and census on the formation of identities of communities in India see Benedict Anderson, *Imagined Communities*, London/New York, 1991, pp. 163–85.

rritorialization of
in popular visual culture

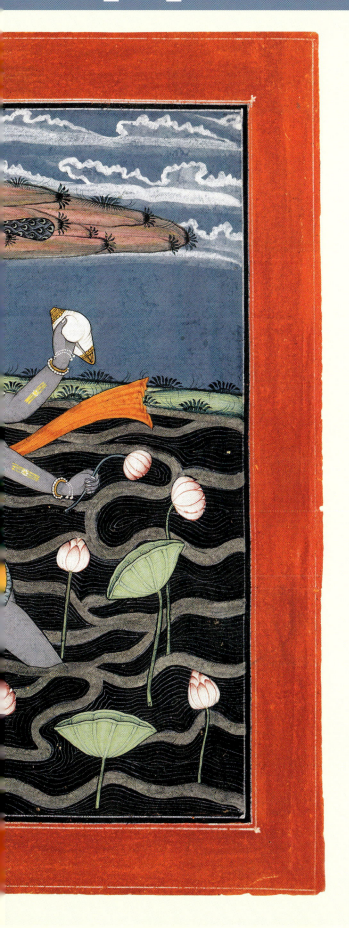

Sumathi Ramaswamy

The sphericity of the globe is not something that comes to us...naturally. It is a residue of cultural activities.... It is hard won knowledge. It is map knowledge.[1]

Europeans delighted in disproving the "wild conceptions of the Poorans"…. True geography… was seen as a way of demolishing heathenism by stealth, and the distribution of globes to schools became a significant aspect of the attempt to spread "useful knowledge".[2]

This is an essay on the contrary uses of cartographic knowledge, on Hindu attempts to enable the passage of their gods into the modern using the very maps and globes introduced by a colonizing empire to release them from "the incubus of superstition"[3] and wean them away from the absurdity of their traditional beliefs. The archive for this essay is idiosyncratic – as befits this kind of contrary cartography – but not without coherency and consistency, despite its episodic and fragmentary state. Constituted by the so-called god-pictures that have been such a ubiquitous feature of the popular visual sphere in India for the past century and more, this archive confirms that a scientific cartographic way of visualizing and seeing can easily coexist with other, especially Puranic, norms of darshan and worship. This archive also demonstrates that even while the gods are literally put in their place on the face of the terrestrial globe and on the map of the emergent nation, scientific cartography itself is hijacked for purposes not intended for it by a rationalizing state with its disenchanting pedagogic and bureaucratic practices. "The program of the Enlightenment", wrote Horkheimer and Adorno famously, "was the disenchantment of the world; the dissolution of myths and the substitution of knowledge for fancy."[4] Yet the contrary manner in which scientific cartography is deployed in the proliferating god-pictures of Hindu India demonstrates how the European Enlightenment project is undone at its (post)-colonial address by the revival of old myths and the return of fancy. Rather than heathenism being demolished, the gods come back even more realistically, exuberantly, and potently, transformed from sectarian "Hindu" deities into nationalized "Indian" divinities through the mediation of the very scientific knowledge that ought

1. (*previous pages*) Varaha avatar, attributed to Mahesh, 1750–75. Folio 3 from a Dashavatar series from Chamba. Opaque watercolour on paper; 16.3 x 24.1 cm. Gift of Balthasar and Nanni Reinhart, Museum Rietberg Zurich, RVI 1514.

2. Varaha rescuing Prithvi. Eran, Madhya Pradesh, late 5th/early 6th century CE. Sandstone. Sagar University Museum, Madhya Pradesh. Photograph courtesy American Institute of Indian Studies, Gurgaon.

3. Varaha avatar. Karla-Lonavla: Ravi Varma Press, late 19th-century? Chromolithograph. Reproduced by permission of the University of Cambridge, Museum of Archaeology and Anthropology, Z 44. 986.

4. Varaha avatar. Statue in temple, Mayapur, Navadvip, Bengal. Google Images.

Varma Press printed a poster that visually recalled this primeval cosmic act (figure 3). The poster shows a blue-grey Varaha – half man, half boar – emerging from the primeval waters, his four hands bearing the standard symbols associated with Vishnu. He is gloriously adorned in jewels, a crown atop his head. But perhaps the most striking feature of this poster is the beautiful terrestrial globe perched on his tusks, the landmasses and oceans marked in astonishing detail. As importantly for the argument I am developing here on cartography's contrary deployment, the globe is centred on the Indian subcontinent, its peninsular outline made familiar by the recent spread of scientific geographic knowledge. The poster seems to suggest that not only is Varaha rescuing Earth, but "India" in particular was saved on this primeval mission. From the perspective of the long representational history of the cosmic act of Varaha rescuing Earth, a history that stretches back to the early 1st millennium CE from when the first sculptures depicting the event have survived (example, figure 2), the poster marks a departure. Prithvi is not shown in her conventional manner as a female divinity – beautiful, demure, and obviously in awe of the immense male animal-god who had saved her from the clutches of the wicked demon. Instead, her sensuous and sentient – and obviously female – body is unambiguously replaced by

to have banished them from the lives and livelihoods of their devotees.

A boar's cartographic adventures

An unusual member of the vast Hindu pantheon of gods is the principal protagonist of this essay. He is Varaha, the third incarnation of Lord Vishnu who took the form of a mighty boar – in the most dominant reckoning as recounted in the Sanskritic Puranas – on a rescue mission to save Earth (Prithvi) from the clutches of the demon Hiranyaksha (figure 2). At the height of colonial modernity – perhaps sometime in the closing years of the 19th century – the newly established Ravi

the inanimate spherical form of the gridded terrestrial globe, the proud invention of the relatively recent science of modern cartography. Puranic cosmology and scientific geography coexist seamlessly and effortlessly with no seeming discomfort over their essential incommensurability.

This poster printed by the Ravi Varma Press – which was quite likely designed by the famous artist himself who started this firm – is not unusual, however, in its displacement of Prithvi by the terrestrial globe: in fact, through the course of the 20th century, this is the dominant manner in which Varaha's cosmic rescue mission is invariably depicted in book illustrations and children's colouring books, in wall paintings on home and temple walls as well as stone statuary (figure 4), in brass plaques, clay toys, and wooden figurines (figure 5), even in the movies and ephemera like *ganjifa* playing cards and board games. The god occasionally does a solo turn (as in figures 3–5), but frequently, Varaha is inserted into paintings, posters, and plaques as part of Vishnu's ten key incarnations, the Dashavatar. For example, in another chromolithograph printed possibly in the early years of the last century also by the Ravi Varma Press, Varaha appears with a terrestrial globe perched on his tusks, the Indian subcontinent once again prominently visible even in this diminutive format (figure 6). A miniaturized Varaha can also be found printed on one of the arms of the multi-armed manifestation of Vishnu as the Lord of the Universe, Vishvarupa or Virat Rupa, another popular subject in this genre. Indeed, we rarely encounter Prithvi as a sensuous goddess being rescued by Varaha in 20th-century art, be it at the high end or in the popular realm: such is the sweep of the displacement of the sentient feminized earth by the inanimate spherical globe of scientific cartography.

Yet, this was not always so, and from at least the mid-17th century, the pictorial representations of Varaha – a popular theme with (Hindu) artists across the subcontinent, especially because of the widespread belief in Vishnu's periodic interventions in the affairs of the mundane world – bear the marks of the struggle on the road to the eventual triumph of the "hard-won knowledge" of the sphericity of Earth.

5. (*facing page*) Varaha avatar. Contemporary wooden figurine from Kondapalli, Andhra Pradesh. Crafts Museum, New Delhi. Photograph courtesy Lee Schlesinger.

6. Dashavatar. Malavli: Anant Shivaji Desai and Ravi Varma Press, early 20th century? Author's personal collection.

REGISTERED 486   अनंत शिवाजी देसाई   दशावतार   भोतीबाजार मुंबई   RAVI VARMA PRESS, MALAVLI, G. I. P.

Just a couple of decades before the publication of the
Ravi Varma Press posters in figures 3 and 6, a Bengali
artist named Krishnahari Das – trained in Calcutta's
newly established School of Art – was commissioned to
provide the illustrations for a printed book on Vishnu's
avatars published in 1880 by Sourindra Mohan Tagore.
In Das's rendering, Earth appears not as a terrestrial
globe but as a hemispheric bowl filled with vegetation
and buildings. In turn, Das's visualization of Varaha –
which is also echoed in some contemporary Bat-tala
woodcuts, and in a Calcutta Art Studio Dashavatar
poster from the 1880s – has a striking resemblance
to a European illustration that first appeared in print
in 1672 in a Dutch publication by Philip Baldaeus
which was subsequently reprinted several times over
the course of the next century, including in English
in 1703 (figure 7).[5] Earth as an inhabited hemispheric
bowl – rather than as a globe mathematically patterned
with the graticule of latitudes and longitudes – also
appears in another Dutch illustration (first printed in
1672) which magnificently combines the Puranic belief
that the world is shouldered on the backs of various
animals with a growing conviction to represent it in
all its glorious sphericity; the female figure in the
illustration has been identified by Olfert Dapper as

Waras of Warrahas *autaer, de derde.*

"the fair dancing maid Remba", but may well be Prithvi herself (figure 8).[6]

Rather than think that printed illustrations like these of Varaha's cosmic act – which appear also in Athanasius Kircher's monumental *China...Illustrata* (1667) and Bernard Picart's important *Ceremonies et coutumes religieuses...des Indes Occidentales* (1723) – are purely European in their inspiration, I would speculate that artists in India may have had a role to play in their initial conceptualization, as Jarl Charpentier tentatively suggested in 1923 when he hinted that "a native convert" based in Surat around 1649–57 might have been the creator of the images that eventually made their way (with alterations) into the manuscripts of Baldaeus and Dapper.[7] Indeed, in Pahari paintings from diverse 18th-century Rajput courts at Kangra, Basohli, Mankot, and Chamba, Varaha invariably appears not with a sensuous Prithvi but with a landmass on which are frequently crowded forests and hills, mansions and temples, and various animals, especially the cow (another form assumed by Earth, in some Puranic stories) (figure 1 and Introduction figure 2). And in a magnificently illustrated manuscript of the *Adhyatma Ramayana* commissioned around 1804, a watercolour in the Patna/Chapra style of Varaha carrying a small slice of earth on his tusk is accompanied by an explanation for the painting's English patron: "After the creation of the world by Brahma, the giant Hirinyacsha rolled up the earth into a shapely mass, and carried it down to the seventh abyss. The God Rama assumed the form of a Boar and having slain the giant he brought up the earth on his tusks, and restored it to Brahma."[8] In the so-called Gentil Album (with paintings commissioned in the 1770s by the French colonel Jean-Baptiste Gentil from artists named Nevasi Lal, Mohan Singh, and others based in and around the north Indian city of Faizabad), Varaha appears with a small globe perched on his tusks.[9] But this is a prescient moment, for in general until the late 19th century, Earth is not unambiguously visualized as an inanimate mathematized and gridded globe in Indian art, although knowledge of it as a spherical entity existed from at least the middle of the 1st millennium CE, if not earlier, among astronomers, providing a rival cosmology to the one enunciated in the Puranas where it was either feminized as a goddess, or imagined as a flat disc or a lotus petal.[10] In illustrations in Sanskrit manuscripts, hand-painted scrolls on cloth, as well as in miniatures commissioned from native artists by Europeans settled in India into the mid-19th century, when Varaha is depicted performing his cosmic act of rescue, the earth generally takes the form of a shapely inhabited landmass sprinkled with forests, hills, mansions, and the occasional animal. In many such visualizations, the animate earth perched on Varaha's tusks resembles the landmass carried across the oceans by Hanuman on his own rescue mission to revive the fallen epic hero Lakshman, or borne by Krishna in his manifestation as Govardhan Giridhar to save earthly inhabitants from the wrath of the rain god Indra. The continued use of such an image on labels used to market modern goods under the aegis of colonial capitalism is apparent from the illustration in figure 9.

As Denis Cosgrove writes in his imaginative study, *Apollo's Eye*, "To imagine the earth as a globe is essentially a visual act... Such a gaze is implicitly imperial, encompassing a geometric surface to be explored and mapped, inscribed with content, knowledge, and authority."[11] To masterfully visualize Earth as an integrated totality, a spherical entity mesmerically suspended in the cosmos and gridded by a mathematical network of latitudes and longitudes, is also an act that requires an enormous leap of imagination that does not come naturally, and has to be learned and in a disciplined manner; as the opening epigram of this essay notes, it is hard-won knowledge, map knowledge. But once such knowledge seizes the human imagination, the image of Earth as a perfect sphere comes to reign, for it is "a figure of enormous imaginative power". As Cosgrove notes, "To achieve the global view is to loose the bonds of the earth, to escape the shackles of time, and to dissolve the contingencies of daily life for a universal moment of reverie and harmony."[12] He also suggests that "desires of ordering and controlling the object of vision" propel the visualization of Earth as globe, and that such desires are "connected as closely to lust for material possession, power and authority as to metaphysical speculation, religious aspiration, or poetic sentiment."[13] Although the sciences of geography

वराह   पराक्रम   वराह

9. Varaha avatar. Goods label, Bombay and Calcutta, early 20th century. Jyotindra Jain Collection, New Delhi.

1. RAMAIAH.
1953

COPYRIGHT
R. ETHIRAJIAH & SONS
MADRAS.3.

BHOODEVI

SOLE PUBLISHERS
R ETHIRAJIAH & SONS,
Madras - 3

COPYRIGHT RESERVED
BY THE PUBLISHERS

10. "Bhoodevi" by
M. Ramaiah, 1953. Madras:
R. Ethirajiah & Sons.
Chromolithograph. Author's
personal collection.

and cartography spread fitfully and incoherently in and across colonial India, globes and the mapped image of the subcontinent as *visual* entities become increasingly visible in the printed public domain from the closing years of the 19th century, and appear in school and college textbooks, on mastheads of journals and newsmagazines, in advertisements and labels for goods, and of course, in poster and calendar art.[14] Yet the embracing of these modern cartographic artefacts – which the colonial educator hoped would wean Hindus away from a dependence on "false" Puranic beliefs – did not lead to a jettisoning of the gods. On the contrary. This is well illustrated in a poster from 1953 titled in English as "Bhoodevi", which shows Earth as a sensuous, sentient, four-armed goddess *and* as a terrestrial globe contained by the graticule of latitudes and longitudes within which the peninsular outline of India is clearly etched (figure 10).[15] Here, as in the Ravi Varma Press poster of Varaha (figure 3), Puranic belief and modern scientific knowledge coexist side by side within the same frame.

Geo-body, divine bodies

In fact, it is not just Varaha or Bhudevi who come to be explicitly associated with the terrestrial globe and the outline map of India, but other gods of the Hindu pantheon as well. They too are "carto-graphed", to coin a neologism.[16] Thus, in a poster published in 1927, and signed by the artist Ghoting, a muscular Hanuman with his trademark club-weapon stands defiantly on a terrestrial globe (not suspended in a mathematized cosmos but immersed in the [primeval?] ocean) on which the outline map of India is clearly inscribed, even showing a couple of its principal rivers; Hanuman's legs straddle the mapped spread of India – its "geo-body" – even as his own body is carto-graphed by the globe and map (figure 11).[17] Similarly, in another poster, published in Ahmedabad, and also titled in English "Brahma Mahesh Vishnu" (with the phrase, "One god in three forms" inscribed in Hindi), the artist T.B. Vathy places the Hindu trinity in the company of a terrestrial globe prominently centred on the Indian geo-body; Shiva's feet are firmly planted on the Indian map, making it his own (figure 12). And in "Bansiwala" (figure 13), Krishna sits firmly on a terrestrial globe on which, once again, the mapped shape of India – its geo-body – is distinctly

pictures suggest that modern mapped knowledge is hijacked to ensure the survival of the gods rather than their exile, even as the gods themselves are used to popularize – among a largely illiterate populace – the otherwise unfamiliar mapped outline of the emergent nation, and the visual image of Earth as an impersonal spherical globe rather than a sentient female or even an animated entity. In other words, rather than science banishing the Puranas, as Christian missionaries and other Enlightened folks had fondly hoped, Puranic knowledge comes in useful for disseminating science's cartographic innovations. In turn, the gods themselves are ontologically transformed. Rather than free-

outlined, his feet resting on a lotus suggestively placed at its southern tip. In all such prints – going back to the earliest years of the 20th century, and continuing into the present – Hinduism's many gods are clearly cartographed, their divine bodies unambiguously locked into the geo-body of the emergent nation, in turn itself a product of recent mapped knowledge. The locking together thus of India's geo-body and Hinduism's many divine bodies is widespread and enduring enough to demand an explanation, especially because of the ubiquity of such imagery in recent Hindu nationalist visual culture where they are submitted to an imminent political agenda of transforming a secular nation-state into a Hindu *rashtra*.

To return then to my opening argument about cartography and its contrary deployments, such

11. (*facing page, left*)
"Shri Hanuman" by
Ghoting, 1927. Bombay:
Anant Shivaji Desai and
Modern Litho Works.
Chromolithograph.
Collection of K.C. Aryan's
Home of Folk Art, Museum
of Folk, Tribal and
Neglected Art, Gurgaon.

12. (*facing page, right*)
"Brahma Mahesh Vishnu"
by T.B. Vathy, mid-20th
century. Ahmedabad:
Chimanlal Chotalal and
Co. Pictures Merchants.
Chromolithograph. Author's
personal collection.

13. "Bansiwala". Artist
unknown, mid-20th
century. Publication
information unknown.
Chromolithograph.
Erwin Neumayer
Collection, Vienna.

Bansiwala

wheeling deities gadding about an uncharted cosmos or wandering around Bharat-varsha and Jambudvipa, they now come to be carto-graphed, their bodies hitched to the terrestrial globe, and locked to the outline map of "India". An entirely innovative way of seeing their gods as earthbound, even India-bound, carto-graphed divinities is thus inaugurated in the subcontinent. Most consequentially, through such a visual and cartographic act, Hindu gods are transformed into *Indian* gods, the geo-body of India nationalizing their divine bodies. With the help of modern cartographic instruments, Hinduism's ancient gods, rather than being irrelevant or redundant, become part of the emergent nation's geo-body, lending it their aura, their powers, and most importantly, their divinity. In turn, India – itself a new-fangled creation of a colonizing power – is sacralized, transformed from any geo-body on the impersonal face of the terrestrial globe into a hallowed land, a *punyabhumi* specially favoured by the gods themselves. Cosgrove notes that the modern terrestrial globe with its geometric grid of latitudes and longitudes "universalises space, privileging no specific point,... extend[ing] a non-hierarchic net across the sphere".[18] Yet, in these god-posters, India appears as the gods' chosen land, centred as these prints are on the outline map of the nation, which frequently appears as the only territory on the earth's surface, and associating as they do the divine bodies of these ancient deities with the modern nation's geo-body.

Most consequentially for the fortunes of a putatively secular polity, it is only the divinities associated with Hinduism – and others such as the Buddha or the Sikh gurus drawn into its cosmology – who are generally associated with the map of India; symbols or figures associated with Islam or Christianity are rarely, if ever, shown in intimate association with the nation's geo-body, appearing generally on the margins of the mapped territory, if not entirely outside it. So, India is not just any land chosen by the gods, but a Hindu land that is the playground of Hindu gods. The putatively secular science of cartography helps consolidate an essentially religious and Hindu view of the nation's geo-body. Such a consolidation reaches its patriotic apogee in the nation's imagination as Bharat Mata, a carto-graphed mother/goddess for whose visual

persona the map of India becomes an essential, even her diagnostic, element.[19] In the early years of the 20th century, Subhas Chandra Bose – the fiery patriot whose nationalist imagination we do not necessarily associate with an essentially Hindu or even religious inflection – wrote: "...India is God's beloved land. He has been born in this great land in every age in the form of the Saviour for the enlightenment of the people, to rid this earth of sin and to establish righteousness and truth in every Indian heart. He has come into being in many other countries in human form but not so many times in any other country – that is why I say, India, our motherland, is God's beloved land...."[20] The popular print culture that flourished in the bazaars and on the streets of the emergent nation and that mass-produced countless numbers of god-posters showing Hinduism's many deities as tangible and meaningful presences in the lives of modern Indians, brought to visual reality this implicit belief that India was indeed God's beloved land, the place to be on the map of the world.

ACKNOWLEDGEMENTS

I want to thank Jyotindra Jain for his comments, as well as my mother Kausalya Ramaswamy for her suggestive reading of this essay.

NOTES

[1] Denis Wood and John Fels, *The Power of Maps*, New York: Guilford Press, 1992, p. 5.

[2] C.A. Bayly, *Empire and Information: Intelligence Gathering and Social Communication in India, 1780–1870*, Cambridge: Cambridge University Press, 1996, p. 301.

[3] George Everest, cited by Matthew H. Edney, *Mapping an Empire: The Geographical Construction of British India, 1765–1843*, Chicago: University of Chicago Press, 1997, p. 312.

[4] Max Horkheimer and Theodor W. Adorno, *Dialectic of Enlightenment*, translated by John Cumming, New York: Seabury, 1972, p. 3.

[5] Awnsham and John Churchill (eds.), *A Collection of Voyages and Travels, Some now First Printed from Original Manuscripts, Others translated out of Foreign Languages, and now first Published in English To which are Added some Few that have formerly appear'd in English, but do now for their Excellency and Scarceness deserve to be reprinted. In Four Volumes with a General Preface, giving an Account*

of the Progress of Navigation, from its first Beginning to the Perfection it is now. The whole Illustrated with a great Number of useful Maps and Cuts, all Engraven on Copper, Vol. 3 (London: Printed for Awnsham and John Churchill at the Black Swan, 1704), p. 849.

6 *Asia, The First Part being An Accurate Description of Persia and the Several Provinces thereof. The Vast Empire of the Great Mogol and other Parts of India: And their Several Kingdoms and Regions: With The Denominations and Descriptions of the Cities, Towns, and Places of Remark therein contain'd. The Various Customs, Habits, Religion, and Languages of the Inhabitants. Their Political Governments, and way of Commerce. Also The Plants and Animals Peculiar to each Country. Collected and Translated from most Authentick Authors, and Augmented with later Observations; Illustrated with Notes, and Adorn'd with peculiar Maps and proper Sculptures* (London: Printed by the Author), facing p. 136.

7 Jarl Charpentier, "The British Museum Ms. Sloane 3290, the Common Source of Baldaeus and Dapper", *Bulletin of the School of Oriental Studies* 3, no. 3 (1923) pp. 413–20. See also Partha Mitter, *Much Maligned Monsters: A History of European Reactions to Indian Art*, Chicago: University of Chicago Press, 1977, Chapter One.

8 India Office Library, Mss Eur C116/1, fol. 10v.

9 Victoria and Albert Museum, London, IS 25-1980, no. 53.

10 I have considered the manner in which the globe form gets incorporated into Mughal art from the early years of the 17th century in "Conceit of the globe in Mughal India", *Comparative Studies in Society and History* 49, no. 4 (2007).

11 Denis Cosgrove, *Apollo's Eye: A Cartographic Genealogy of the Earth in Western Imagination*, Baltimore: Johns Hopkins University Press, 2001, pp. 15–16.

12 Ibid., p. 3.

13 Ibid., p. 5.

14 Sumathi Ramaswamy, "Visualizing India's Geo-Body: Globes, Maps, Bodyscapes", in Sumathi Ramaswamy (ed.), *Beyond Appearances? Visual Practices and Ideologies in Modern India*, New Delhi: Sage, 2003, pp. 157–95.

15 General Editor's Note: This image of Bhudevi is interesting as she carries three of Vishnu's attributes which normally Bhudevi does not. The image also suggests the emergent idea of Bharat Mata.

16 On the basis of a dictionary understanding of cartography as the drawing of maps, I have coined the neologism "carto-graphed" to underscore the manner in which human and divine bodies are drawn to reproduce, accommodate, or outline the map form.

17 Thongchai Winichakul introduces the term "geo-body" to refer to the entirely novel way of representing territory in modernity as bounded wholes through the sciences of geography and cartography (*Siam Mapped: A History of the Geo-Body of Nation*, Honolulu: University of Hawaii Press, 1994).

18 *Apollo's Eye*, pp. 105–06.

19 Sumathi Ramaswamy, "Visualizing India's Geo-Body". Globes, Maps, Bodyscapes".

20 Subhas Chandra Bose. "Mother India" (1912–13), in *The Essential Writings of Netaji Subhas Chandra Bose*, edited by Sisir K. Bose and Sugata Bose, Delhi: Oxford University Press, 1997, pp. 19–22; see p. 20.

"THE ACCIDENTAL RAMDEV"

Christopher Pinney

the spread of a popular cult

सुगबाई   श्री रामदेव जी महाराज   रलीबाई

There are several forces that incline accounts of popular Indian art towards an inevitability. Mass-produced pictures are assumed to be "popular" in a demographic sense. Often this is well founded because they are produced, and usually consumed, in large numbers. Tied to this is the prevailing strategy of taking visual evidence as a sign of some underlying force. As signs, images are imputed a fullness: "emptiness" and contingency are much harder to establish. Further, what Carlo Ginzburg, following E.H. Gombrich, describes as "physiognomic" circularity is very hard to escape. Images, despite what their analysts might claim, are usually deployed as illustrations of an argument that has already been established "by other means".[1]

In this article I will explore a genre of images of one particular deity, whose appearance might be understood to be accidental, the result of haphazard, indeed almost random migration between different spheres of cultural production. The deity with whom I am concerned is Ramdevji, a Rajasthani figure who is now widely worshipped through north and western India. He is a warrior-hero, of the kind which is sometimes generically described as *bhomiya*.[2] Ramdevji emerges from a regional Rajasthani pantheon where he shares many features with other figures such as Gogaji, Dev Narayan, Pabuji, and Tejaji.

Ramdevji is a figure around whom many diverse narratives cohere. Some parts of his story are presented within the frame of a universal history: he was born a Tomar Rajput in 1408 and achieved samadhi (voluntary abandonment of his mortal body) in 1458. For many Hindus he was an avatar of Krishna, for Muslims he is Ramshah Pir. Dominique-Sila Khan has argued (controversially) that he embodies the residue of an Ishmaeli ecumenicalism.[3] Whatever the facts, he is a product of a highly cosmopolitan society in which complex Rajasthani folk traditions intersected with Shia and other practices. However, above and beyond debates around his specific community identity and location, the main base of devotion in contemporary India celebrates him for his radical anti-caste and anti-hierarchical practices. He is especially popular among Dalit and Adivasi groups for his espousal of an ethical polity.[4] He is the ideal moral ruler, the king

who rescues imprisoned tribals, who (in one reading of narratives associated with him) accepts water from a Chamar, and mixes with pirs as *bhai-bhai*. Folk narratives continually stress his egalitarian ethos, and his intervention against injustice associated with hierarchy.

For the rural Madhya Pradesh Dalits with whom I've worked since the 1980s, Ramdev embodies the utopia of just rule: a renunciatory raja who pays scrupulous ethical attention to injustices within his polity. Dalit devotion to the cult of Ramdev cedes political autonomy to a kingly agency who is entrusted with the responsibility of ethical justice, a theme to which various oral and printed narratives, and chromolithographic visualizations of Ramdev, pay special attention.[5] The prominence of Ramdev – a figure associated with a very precise locality in Rajasthan – in the consciousness of those who live in other parts of India is due, I want to argue, to his almost "accidental" dissemination through the medium of chromolithography.

1. (*previous pages*) "*Shri Harji ke Ramdevji Maharaj*". Chromolithograph by Harnarayan and Sons, Bombay. Artist: B.G. Sharma, early 1950s. Collection of Hemant Narayan.

2. Bihari, a Malwa Dalit, with a framed copy of B.G. Sharma's "*Ramdevji ki Samadhi*". Photograph: Christopher Pinney.

In one Madhya Pradesh village, surveyed in the 1990s, there were 33 images of Ramdev displayed in village homes. Five of these images were to be found in Rajput households to whom the figure of a Rajput king appeals. Small numbers of images were also to be found in Brahman, Gujar, and Banjara households, but it is in Chamar homes – where there were 13 – that the largest number of Ramdevji pictures can be found (figure 2). Although it is frequently claimed that figures like Ramdevji are revered by all castes, it is also simultaneously acknowledged that Chamars have a greater belief in Ramdevji (*chamar zyada mante*). The clearly articulated reason for this is Ramdevji's egalitarianism and opposition to caste inequality and untouchability, made explicitly clear in the narrative associated with him.

In reconstructing this "accidental" lineage the publishers Harnarayan and Sons – founded in Jodhpur in 1929 – will play a major role. Like the Brijbasi brothers (who would quickly come to dominate the pan-Indian picture market) Harnarayan Mehra had run a picture-framing business before deciding to publish his own images. He had in fact first worked on the railways as an apprentice carpenter before turning his woodworking skills to frame-making. His company's first print, dated May 1929, was the result of a visit to Nathdvara to commission Pushtimarg artists, again following the Brijbasi pattern. Some of Harnarayan's earliest images echo those of Brijbasi, for example Narottam Narayan's studies of Krishna as Gopal appearing through apocalyptic clouds. Narottam's output also mixed a similar blend of portraits of Gandhi and Nehru with more orthodox religious images. But Harnarayan's images also reflected a very regionally specific concern with figures in the Rajasthani pantheon.

An insight into the western Rajasthani milieu within which Harnarayan operated is provided by a 1930s image of Sardar Market in Jodhpur, painted by the Nathdvara artist A. Girdharilal, and published by Harnarayan. The huge fort – the citadel of Marwar – is depicted towering over Jodhpur city at the centre of which lies Sardar Market with its tall clock tower. A couple of awnings protect shopfronts from the sun,

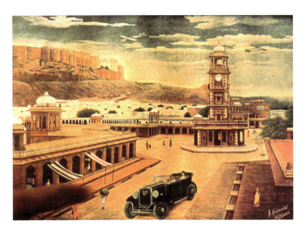

3: "Sardar Market" painted by Girdharilal and published by Harnarayan and Sons, Jodhpur, 1930s. Harnarayan's son Hemant's finger, in the lower left corner, is pointing to his father whom the artist has depicted seated in the car. Collection of Hemant Narayan. Photograph: Christopher Pinney.

4. Detail of figure 3 showing Harnarayan sitting in the back of his Austin Six. Collection of Hemant Narayan. Photograph: Christopher Pinney.

and half a dozen people amble around the largely empty streets. In the sky, improbably, two planes circle overhead, but the main focus of the image is an unfeasibly large Austin Six. The open-topped, chauffeured vehicle transports no less than Harnarayan himself in regal opulence through the streets of his town (figures 3 and 4).

What we might think of as a "Jodhpuri weltanschauung" is evident in the output of the press that Harnarayan ran. In the Sardar Market print a small road can be seen winding its way below the fort. A left turn on that road would put the traveller on the main route west to Jaisalmer, and halfway along that road lies Ramdevra, the site of Ramdev's samadhi.

The company's reference prints (retained by Harnarayan's son Hemant in Bombay) reveal that almost half of the press's early output (from 1929 to c. 1940) were images of Ramdevji, represented either through scenes of his samadhi (at Ramdevra), or as Maharaj-ji, seated on his horse, in kingly profile. In both the samadhi and maharaj genres, Ramdevji is always

श्रीराम देवजी महाराज

हरजी भाटी

डाली बाई

). COPY RIGHT NO 4596

हरनारायण एन्ड सन्स जोधपुर
AT. KHANVILKAR L. P.

श्रीरामदेवजी महाराज

5. *"Shri Ramdevji Maharaj"*. Chromolithograph published by Harnarayan and Sons, Jodhpur, c. 1930. Collection of Hemant Narayan.

6. Ramdev's samadhi. Harnarayan and Sons, Jodhpur, May 1929. Collection of Hemant Narayan.

situated at the centre of the image, and is flanked by two figures. These figures are Harji, who usually appears on the left, and Dalibai, usually on the right. Shortly I will have more to say about the specific roles they play in Ramdevji mythology; here I will simply underline the ways in which they replicate the positions occupied by devotees in the genre of Nathdvara images known as *manoratha*s. In these images, devotees are shown symmetrically flanking the central deity.

The inflexible replication of the *manoratha* composition is not the only "archaic" feature of Harnarayan's Ramdevji genre. Equally striking is the fact that in these early images Ramdevji is always shown in profile, usually facing right, but occasionally facing left. This reflects Ramdevji's rural origins as a warrior hero who – before the advent of chromolithography – would have been worshipped through pressed metal and clay profile images.[6] Shortly we will examine some later images in which Ramdevji's archaic profile is reoriented into an oblique space that brings him closer to the face-to-face darshanic convention of most chromolithographic production.

The earliest Harnarayan Ramdev image was also the first print that Harnarayan produced when he decided the move from mere picture-framing to picture publishing. Its subject matter has a certain logic: it depicts Ramdevji's samadhi in Ramdevra (figure 6). The logic here relates to proximity (Ramdevra was a couple of hours away in Harnarayan's Austin Six). However, the print also appeared at the time that Maharaja Ganga Singh of Bikaner was upgrading the Ramdevra temple. Ganga Singh's improvements were complete by 1931. Harnarayan's Ramdev samadhi image was dated May 1929. A small print (20 x 15 cm) it depicts the samadhi with a rigorous frontality: the marble floor, escutcheons, railings, *chattri*s, and drapes of the temple are depicted in an uncompromisingly rectilinear form.

This same rigour is apparent in Harnarayan's second image, "*Shri Ramdevji Maharaj*", a figure which itself would soon be incorporated into the background of the Ramdevra samadhi which the previous print described. In "*Shri Ramdevji Maharaj*", printed at the Khanvilkar Litho Press, Ramdevji is shown on horseback in profile in a manner similar to that of other Rajasthani warrior heroes such as Dev Narayan and Gogaji (figure 5). Two supplementary figures are also established who will endure through to the present: Harji Bhati, his male follower who stands

to the left with a peacock fan and flywhisk, and Dalibai who worships him on the right with *dipa*s. This image seems to be a close copy of an earlier image published by another Jodhpur Press, a copy of which was held in Hemant Mehra's company files. This earlier image, "*Shri Ramdevji Ramsapir*" dates from 1920 and was published by Achalu Pratap Nyayi and Company (figure 7). The copy in the Harnarayan files is very poorly printed – suffering from misalignment of the different litho stones. One can imagine the picture-framer Harnarayan seeing the appearance of this poorly printed picture and perhaps sensing that it would have appeal but would deter people by its poor execution. We can imagine him thinking how a crisper, more alluring colour lithograph would appeal to a wider audience. "*Shri Ramdevji Maharaj*" was essentially a technically superior reworking of Nyayi's earlier image, but it also – perhaps crucially – marked a Hinduization of Ramdev. Rather than "Ramsapir" he now became Maharaj, no longer so obviously a figure of the religious frontier: now he was more explicitly tagged as the ideal ruler of the Hindu polity.

7. "*Shri Ramdevji Ramsapir*". Chromolithograph published by Achalu Pratap Nyayi and Company, Jodhpur, 1920. Collection of Hemant Narayan.

RAMDEVJI KI GURU BHET
711
PRINTED AT HAR NARAYAN ART PRINTING
WORKS

8. "*Ramdevji ki Guru Bhet*". Chromolithograph published by Harnarayan and Sons, Jodhpur. Artist: "D.L.", c. 1935. Collection of Hemant Narayan.

9. "*Ramdevji Samadhi*". Chromolithograph published by Harnarayan and Sons, Bombay, c. 1950. Collection of Hemant Narayan.

168 रामदेवजी समाधि

HARNARAYAN & SONS
335, Kalbadevi Road, BOMBA

A slightly later Harnarayan image – "*Ramdevji ki Guru Bhet*" fleshes out further narrative elements of the Ramdevji myth (figure 8). The image focuses on Ramdev's encounter with Shribalaknathji Guru who we see seated to the left centre of the picture, and the narrative complexity of the image is again framed by the flanking presence of Harji Bhati and Dalibai. Ramdev is presented in the familiar profile but reversed so that he faces left.

"*Ramdevji ki Guru Bhet*" seems not to have sold well. Its narrative was too obscure and complex, and subsequent Harnarayan images relegate it to a vignette within a larger image. "*Ramdevji Samadhi*", produced in the early 1950s from Harnarayan's Bombay office (figure 9), elaborates and further enfleshes the Ramdevra image with which Harnarayan had first broken into the mass picture-production in 1929 (see figure 6). We see Ramdevji's samadhi at the centre of the image, and the same drapes and *chhatri*s contained in the earlier image. But in "*Ramdevji Samadhi*" we see signs of the development of the shrine. Oval portraits of the Bikaner royal family record their contribution to the redevelopment of the shrine, and chromolithographically disseminated signs of the cult are reintegrated as part of the decor of the shrine. Most importantly we see at the centre of the image, hung on the railing behind the samadhi image, the key icon of Ramdev on horseback in profile. The image which

10. (*above right*) "*Ramdevji ki Samadhi*". Chromolithograph published by Sharma Picture Publications, Bombay, mid-1950s. Author's collection.

11. "*Shriramdevjiki Jivanlila*". Chromolithograph published by Harnarayan and Sons, early 1950s. Collection of Hemant Narayan.

Harnarayan had earlier published as "*Ramdevji ki Guru Bhet*" appears as a very small framed print hanging on the far right wall. The whole ensemble is framed by devotees – Dalibai on the left and Harji on the right, with the addition of four other figures framing the image symmetrically.

"*Ramdevji Samadhi*" is printed in the vibrant colours which would later come to be associated with B.G. Sharma, the Nathdvara artist who – with his brother – would found Sharma Picture Publications in the mid-1950s. B.G. (Bhanwarlal Girdharilal) Sharma was the son of Girdharilal, the artist who painted "*Sardar Market*". Following in his father's footsteps, B.G. Sharma produced more than a dozen designs for Harnarayan before revolutionizing the picture industry with his vibrant palette.

It is possible that "*Ramdevji Samadhi*" is the work of B.G. Sharma. In any event in the 1950s B.G. Sharma would become one of the key visual interpreters of Ramdevji, consolidating existing iconography and extending it in an experimental fashion. Of Sharma's images, five are worthy of comment. Two of them are essentially reworkings and elaborations of pre-established images, and three of them attempt something quite new. The two which fall into the first category, "*Ramdevji ki Jivanlila*" and "*Ramdevji ki Samadhi*" further develop templates with which we are already very familiar: Ramdev's samadhi at Ramdevra, and the profile of the horse-borne Ramdev (figures 10 and 12). What B.G. Sharma brings to these is a hugely more complex intensification of the narrative elements which frame both images. In the samadhi image we see many more pictures within the picture.

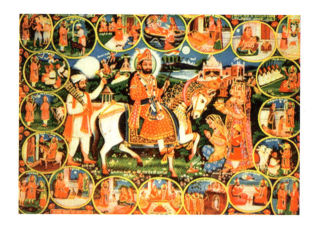

The images which depict episodes from Ramdev's life are placed within pictures of the *chardham* (four places of pilgrimage) and along the top of the image we see Ramdev's father Ajmal, Ramdev's meeting with Harji, his encounter with the five pirs (*panch pir*), and so on. This density of biographical narrative is made even more complex in B.G. Sharma's quite remarkable *jivanlila*[7] image in which the warrior Ramdev in profile is completely enclosed in a frame of medallions within which a very full visual exposition of his life is presented. Significantly, some versions of this print were released with the title "*Ramdevji ki Arati*", directing our attention to the way in which these yellow-ringed "flames" that contain the narrative episodes were to be viewed in a circular fashion not only for their pedagogical recounting of Ramdev's life and deeds, but also for the physical effect of *arati* that the image could produce. Harnarayan had published a *jivanlila* image (figure 11) sometime before Sharma's own image appeared with Sharma Picture Publications. This image is rather mysterious: it bears the logo "*Rajasthan Chitrashala*" (under Harji Bhati's name), suggesting that it may have been the work of another press reissued by Harnarayan. There is no indication of the artist but it is possible that this is the work of a very young B.G. Sharma – or an entirely different artist.

This Harnarayan *jivanlila* contains sixteen medallions visualizing Ramdev's "proofs", and the samadhi image (top left corner) is strikingly similar to the very first image issued by Harnarayan (see figure 6). B.G. Sharma's *jivanlila* contains twenty *parcha*s or "proofs", shows Ramdev facing right and deploys a less-restrained palette (see figure 12). Sharma's work, like much else produced by Sharma Picture Publications would sweep

all before it. An increasingly rural audience for these images embraced the vibrancy of their colours, and the pastoralist and peasant visual world which this urbane Nathdvara Brahman was able to convey so powerfully.

The innovatory images Sharma produced give a strong sense of an entrepreneurial artist continually striving to develop new iconography and subtly transform his aesthetic regime, at the very moment that he also seeks to respect the tradition with which he is working. This modification within established parameters is a key feature of a commercial industry of picture production which is very conscious of

12. (*left*) "*Ramdevji ki Jivanlila*". Chromolithograph published by Sharma Picture Publications, Bombay. Artist: B.G. Sharma, mid-1950s. Author's collection.

13. Chromolithograph published by Harnarayan and Sons, Bombay. Collection of Hemant Narayan.

the conservatism of its customer base, and whose valorization of its own products as intrinsically transcendent also imposes its own constraints.

Within these limits we can see how Sharma emphasizes and de-emphasizes aspects of a pre-existing repertoire. This is especially clear in "*Shri Harji ke Ramdevji Maharaj*", a fascinating early 1950s image which, as its title indicates, gives Harji a much greater prominence than earlier images (figure 1). It is also the only image I have ever encountered in which Ramdev is not shown mounted on his horse. Harji is present in all Ramdevji images, both in episodes that act as *parcha*s, and within the main part of the image – usually shown

standing behind Ramdev holding a flywhisk. Various stories circulate about Harji: according to one of them Ramdev met Harji – who was then a goatherder – and being thirsty asked him for water.

In this image – perhaps intended to appeal to the Meghwal devotees of Ramdev – Harji is made into the principal *chela* (disciple) and has acquired an iconography reminiscent of Tukaram and Kabir. He plays a simple tanpura, and holds thumb cymbals in his left hand. In this image we see a commercial artist speculatively proposing a new form of devotion to Harji – one which failed (as it happened) to materialize: I have seen no other images which give such prominence to Harji.

Another of Sharma's innovations repositioned Ramdev from the enduring Rajasthani template into a new cinematically created chronotope. This is best exemplified by two images, one of which is probably Sharma's work, the other of which certainly is. The first of these is known to me only through a damaged Harnarayan file print which lacks the title (figure 13). As with the other image which B.G. Sharma has confirmed is his work, one can imagine a film camera on a boom moving towards the earlier images of Ramdevji in profile. The camera swings to the left, circling behind Harji, and continuing its clockwise movement, comes to rest on the opposite side from where it started. The camera's lens is raised slightly higher than it started and presents the ensemble of Ramdev, Harji, and Dalibai in a new cinematic, three-dimensional space. Ramdev is now presented to us obliquely, moving out towards the left, and embodying a corporeal volume wholly lacking in the earlier images.

The second image in which we see this transformation was initially published by Harnarayan who then sold the rights to Jain Picture Publishers. B.G. Sharma subsequently published a very similar image through his own Sharma Picture Publications, but with the amended title "*Ramdevji ka Choubis Parcha*", although – paradoxically – the image only depicts eighteen "proofs" (figure 14).

B.G. Sharma's third innovation lay in his merging

14. "*Ramdevji ka Choubis Parcha*". Chromolithograph published by Sharma Picture Publications, Bombay. Artist B.G. Sharma, mid-1950s. Author's collection.

of sati imagery with that of Ramdev. Both of course speak to enduring Rajasthani preoccupations but to my knowledge this was the first and last time that they were united in a single image. Much popular picture production involves pastiche and the recycling of elements and this is explicitly apparent in this case. Sharma had produced a successful Satimata image for Kishan Narayan in 1954[8] and we can imagine the publisher encouraging Sharma to combine that image with his longer established Ramdevji work. "*Satimata Ramdevji*" depicted that same cinematically refigured Ramdev that I have just described, advancing towards the immolating Sati (figure 15). Among the gods hovering in the sky are members of the Bikaner royal family, and Jodhpur's new Umaid Bhawan palace (completed in 1944) is depicted on the far left of the picture. This sign of Indo-deco decadence may seem

incongruous. However, its origins as a famine-relief exercise started in 1929 following three monsoon failures casts it in a rather different light: indeed Bhupendra Singh of Bikaner who appears top right, second from right, is positioned directly above Ramdev as though to suggest a homology between Ramdev's ethical politics and those of the then current Raja.

Ramdev imagery was not the sole preserve of Girdharilal and B.G. Sharma. In the 1940s, the artist L.A. Joshi published an image "*Shri Ramdev Pir*" which presented the familiar profile image of the warrior (figure 16). Other publishers produced images in the 1960s and '70s. J.B. Khanna's "*Ramdev Ji*" juxtaposed the warrior image with an equal sized samadhi and reduced the profusion of events in the Sharma *arati* image to six. Film producers also

15. "*Satimata Ramdevji*". Chromolithograph published by Harnarayan and Sons, Bombay. Artist B.G. Sharma, early 1950s. Author's collection.

श्री रामदेवजी महाराज

किशननारायण एन्ड सन्स जोध

16. *"Shri Ramdev Pir"*. Chromolithograph published by Joshi Art Works. Artist: L.A. Joshi, early 1940s. Author's collection.

cashed in on Ramdevji's popularity, Vinod Kumar of Sima Films (Jodhpur) producing *Baba Ramdev Pir* and Vallabh Choksi directing *Jai Baba Ramdev*. These low-budget productions transpose the aesthetics of *katha* performances to film, but marketed as VCDs and music CDs they cloak themselves in imagery which by now will be extremely familiar (figure 17 and Introduction figure 3).

This describes one arc of a circle: traditional Ramdev imagery moved from highly stereotypical images on clay tablets and silver talismans into chromolithography in the 1920s. As the tradition of chromolithographic depictions of Ramdev developed, his representation was subtly transformed. Transformed into a further medium – film, he seems in many ways to revert to the traditional icon which has endured over many centuries. A similar circularity is apparent in the manner in which the images I have discussed above are sometimes used as visual aides to oral narration. Travelling bards are to be found at religious fairs and wander from village to village, singing the songs of their lord and using a framed chromolithograph (in the case of figure 2, B.G. Sharma's *"Ramdevji ki Samadhi"*) in much the same way that *bhopas* refer to Pabuji *par*s.[9]

Conclusion

The study of Ramdevji's mechanically reproduced career raises two points that I believe to be significant for the broader study of India's popular visual culture. The first of these concerns the accidental and haphazard nature of Ramdevji's ascent. Had Harnarayan chosen to commission chromolithographs of other Rajasthani folk-heroes, such as Dev Narayan, or Pabuji, it is my contention that they may well have come to find

17. Inlay card of VCD of Sima Films' *Baba Ramdev Pir*. Author's collection.

new north Indian publics in the way that Ramdevji has. Of course one would want to factor in particular narrational aspects of the Ramdevji story here: his anti-caste message has surely been of importance in the spread of his appeal among Dalits. However, the fact remains that histories of popular picture production will always find it difficult to fully exclude a teleological substrate which assumes a certain inevitability about the success of certain divine figures and not of others. My suggestion here is that without the confluence of Harnarayan's presence in Jodhpur and the Bikaner royal family's investment in the Ramdevra shrine in the late 1920s, Ramdevji might not have found chromolithographic fame, and would not now be the significant deity that he is in much of western and northern India. We can think about this question of contingency in another way: recently, several publishers have produced images of another Rajasthani warrior-hero, Gogaji (e.g. Paradise publisher's *"Jahar Vir Gogaji"*, figure 18). These images are iconographically extremely similar to those of the Ramdevji tradition which I have described here. Gogaji is shown on a horse which is in profile, although he turns to face the viewer. He is flanked by disciples – Bhajju Kotaval and Rani Sariyal – who look very similar to Harji and Dalibai, and his "proofs" are shown in *arati*-like medallions. Perhaps in 50 years a future historian of Gogaji images will be

able to describe a trajectory similar to the one I have here outlined for Ramdev.

The second conclusion may appear at first sight to be of very modest dimensions, but I would like to suggest that it opens up a much greater set of issues. I have commented on Ramdevji images' replication of the *manoratha* convention which have accompanied that other archaic dimension of Ramdevji's mechanically reproduced afterlife: his depiction largely in profile in a way that sustains enduring Rajasthani techniques. The tenacity of this archaic scheme in an age of industrial gods may seem paradoxical. But the case of Shrinathji (of whom Harnarayan also produced images) suggests that there is no disjuncture between the continuation of tried and tested schemata, and the revolutionary transformation of India's dominant scopic regime during the 20th century. The Nathdvara

18. *"Jahar Vir Gogaji"*. Chromolithograph published by Paradise. Unknown artist, 2005. Author's collection.

revolution largely precipitated by S.S. Brijbasi but in which Harnarayan also undeniably played a small part, dislodged Ravi Varma's "absorptive" paradigm and replaced it with a "theatrical" darshanic regime in which devotees could look directly at the full faces of gods who reciprocated their visual devotion. Nathdvara artists, trained to paint pichhvais and images of Shrinathji, once they were commissioned by Brijbasi, and Harnarayan, made a tradition evolved over two centuries in the context of wealthy havelis available to a much broader audience. This full-frontal darshanic idiom mobilized the spaces first created by theatre and then by cinema and became what we might (after Pierre Bourdieu) call the "dominant-class" aesthetic. But these same artists also reproduced a different kind of aesthetic expressive of a more marginal figure who continued to live on the fringes of society. He occupied the desert rather than the haveli, and was expressed through a *katha* aesthetic, rather than through the darshanic.[10] Ramdevji's elevation to a figure of mass culture may have been accidental, but he remains a figure positioned within the margins. Whereas darshanic figures of Lakshmi or Krishna are appealed to for material benefit in a largely narration-less world, for Dalit and other followers of Ramdevji, he remains a figure of action, whose profile directs attention to his *jivanlila*. This *lila* is not simply a demonstration of his power, and hence the reason why he should be worshipped. It is, rather, pedagogic: his aesthetic reveals itself to be an ethic, recoverable through the study of his narrative, to which his enduring profile continually directs us.

NOTES

[1] Carlo Ginzburg, "From Aby Warburg to E.H. Gombrich: A Problem of Method", in *Clues, Myths and the Historical Method*, Baltimore: Johns Hopkins University Press, 1989, p. 35.

[2] See Rustom Bharucha, *Rajasthan: An Oral History, Conversations with Komal Kothari*, Delhi: Penguin Books, 2003, pp. 307ff.

[3] Dominique-Sila Khan, *Conversions and Shifting Identities: Ramdev Pir and the Ismailis in Rajasthan*, Delhi: Manohar, 1997.

[4] In Rajasthan his traditional devotional base has been among Meghwals.

[5] As one popular text puts it *us madhya mein shri ramdevji maharaja ne kiya vahi updesh aur vahi marg is bisavin shatabdi mahatma Gandhi ne kiya* (Mahatma Gandhi advocated the same path and direction in the 20th century as Ramdevji did in his time). Swami Mahatma Gokuldasji Maharaja, *Shriramdevji maharaja ke jama jagaran vidhi*, Ajmer, n.d., p. 10 of Preface.

[6] See Julia and David Eliott, *Gods of the Byways: Wayside Shrines of Rajasthan, Madhya Pradesh and Gujarat*, Oxford: Museum of Modern Art, 1982.

[7] The same print was occasionally also issued under the title *Ramdevji Choubis Parcha* (Ramdev's twenty-four proofs), although this was more commonly used as the title for a portrait-format image showing Ramdev in an oblique angle (see discussion below).

[8] Illustrated in Christopher Pinney, *Photos of the Gods*, London: Reaktion, 2004, p. 153.

[9] See Kavita Singh "To Show, To See, To Tell, To Know: Patuas, Bhopas, and their Audiences" in Jyotindra Jain (ed.) *Picture Showmen: Insights into the Narrative Tradition in Indian Art*, Mumbai: Marg Publications, 1998, pp. 100–15.

[10] The distinction between darshanic and *katha* images is made by O.P. Joshi in *Gods of Heaven, Home of Gods: A Study of Popular Prints*, Jaipur: Illustrated Book Publishers, 1994, pp. 4–6, 9–11.

Anuradha Kapur

Front curtain

The word "curtain" is somewhat imprecisely defined in theatre practice and is in the main understood to mean "the large wall of fabric folds that closes the opening of the proscenium", says Richard Southern in his celebrated book *Changeable Scenery*.[1] This curtain, in some senses obligatory to the very architecture of the proscenium arch theatre, is usually associated with closure or disclosure: and among its most predictable conventions is the one linked with the opening or closing of a performance. The front curtain, even today, rises at the start of a play, and remains up until the last dialogue has been delivered, when it falls to mark the end of the show.

Also called the proscenium curtain, it may have little or even nothing to do with the scene that it shuts in or opens out. It can therefore be understood as part of the "furnishing" of the theatre.[2] It may be made of velvet and decorated with braids and tassels, as is often the case in elaborate or sophisticated theatres, or it may simply be a single-colour cloth, like the unmistakable green fabric that opened and closed the stage aperture in 17th-century England.[3] It might behave in one of several different ways: "it may draw from the sides, fall inwards from the corners where it was bunched up in festoons, or drop vertically from above".[4]

Act Drop

Some curtains inaugurate the play by revealing the mise en scene, but others, while they do have a family tie with the front curtain in that they are used to *close* the picture window of the stage, are dissimilar in appearance; that is, they are not a plain wall of fabric and are instead painted. These are called Act Drops and are, as the name suggests, dropped at the end of

1. (*previous pages*) A still from the play *Chandipriya*, staged by Surabhi Theatre. Raja Vasanta Rao hands over Chandipriya, his unwanted female child, to his Minister Ravi Varma to discard her.

2. A still from the play *Chandipriya*, staged by Surabhi Theatre. Raja Vasanta Rao orders his Minister to kill all newborn females in the kingdom.

each act to facilitate complex scene changes, as well as give a sense of closure to the sequence of the story. The image on the Act Drop functions as a herald or legend of the company and was meant to publicize the company's attractions. As Kathryn Hansen points out, the drop of the Gaiety Theatre in Bombay, which was built by C.S. Nazir in 1879, was supervised by the Governor Sir Richard Temple. The image preferred was one that emphasized "civic pride": "a fine view of Back Bay with the new public buildings – of which the High Courts, the Clock Tower, and the Secretariat are the most prominent – from Malabar Point". The Novelty Theatre, "Constructed by the Victoria Company's owners Baliwala and Moghul in 1887...featured a drop scene by the German painter Maurice Freyberger".[5]

However diverse the temperaments of these methods of disclosure (or closure), the painted scenery or cloth revealed at the *back* of the proscenium curtain or the Act Drop is the one that actually launches the narrative. This curtain, in its several materializations, is the subject of this essay.

Drop scene

Beyond or behind the proscenium curtain, the acts and scenes are set up like a deck of cards; through them the story is sequenced and the narrative organized. Each scene within an act materializes by dropping curtains with distinctive painted locales that descend vertically or are flown down from the flies onto the stage. Not intended to close off a picture encased within the frame of the stage by shutting the proscenium opening like the front curtain does, the painted drop is placed in such a way *within* the proscenium arch, in any one of several positions preset for a back scene, that it leaves a wide acting area in front that is manifestly for the

3. A still from the play *Chandipriya*, staged by Surabhi Theatre. Sage Narada approaches Parvati to give right sense to Raja Vasanta Rao who has ordered the killing of all newborn females in the kingdom.

actors to perform on, so that depending on the way you look at it, the actors are always either *against* the curtain, or *before* it. The actors are, as it were, revealed *nested* within the painted scene.

Hollow surround

Curtains drew the gaze of the spectator to themselves and developed, on the principles of optical convergence, *sides* – four pairs of wings – and then, eventually, a *top* – sky borders – to complete what Richard Southern calls a "hollow surround"[6] with,

also, a *back scene* representing typically an image in perspective.[7] Thus a painted landscape may have had appropriately illustrated wings angled in such a way as to direct attention toward the receding centre of a picture with clouds and sky painted on the top borders to complete the alcove of the stage in which the actor was enclosed.

The experience of a dazzling transformation achieved by a plunging curtain that altered in an instant the stage picture became a crowd-puller in

4. A still from the play *Chandipriya*, staged by Surabhi Theatre. Chandipriya, who was secretly brought up by the Minister of Raja Vasanta Rao and has mastered archery, comes in disguise to the King and splits a palm into two with a single arrow.

5. A still from the play *Chandipriya*, staged by Surabhi Theatre. Chandipriya defies Raja Vasanta Rao's command to get married and declares her wish to go to Kashi.

18th- and 19th-century England,[8] and remains, to this day, the most extraordinary nuts-and-bolts technology that has been attempted for instance by the Surabhi Company to very flamboyant effect.

Stage anatomy

The precise anatomy of the proscenium we take for granted today – with the performer positioned decisively *within* the frame – came into existence in Europe and England in the late 18th century, and culminated architecturally, in England, for example, when a moulded and gilded border was fixed around the Haymarket arch in 1880 to make the stage unmistakably like a picture.[9] The projecting edge of a platform, also called the forestage (or apron) had been shortened so as to be pushed back into the shell of the theatre and in its place was put the orchestra pit which is still to be found in more or less the same position across the world even if in different manifestations.

The typical Victorian-picture-frame stage then was a rectangular proscenium opening with sizeable wing space on either side to deposit and convey furniture, scenery pieces, and props onto the stage. A fly system able to accommodate the vertical rise of curtains to the extent that they remained out of sight was also created. In these concealed spaces the elements that created the magic of stage illusion were stored. On top were pulleys and counterweights to draw up and plunge down curtains and scenery, and under the stage, often to the depth of 10 metres, were traps and slits for actors to be propelled upwards or delivered downwards into pits, or graves, or other netherworlds. Even today the Surabhi Company constructs a stage more or less on these lines, albeit in an abbreviated form, and instead of a gilded frame mounts a decorated border atop its theatre to reproduce as it were a picture frame.

Such is also the stage that the Parsi Theatre fabricated after Indian audiences became enamoured of the proscenium arch and its possibilities.[10] Indeed the proscenium arch, brought to India by the British in the 1750s and promoted thereafter, replaced the open stage that had been the most prevalent performing site up to this time and prompted an elaborate change in the

theatrical expectations of the viewing public. What the audiences looked forward to was stage illusion (which is also by a curious process of morphing, fabulous stage artifice) made possible by the "rationalized visual system"[11] of the proscenium arch with its perspectival arrangements that tricked the eye, by the angled wings and the painted vanishing point that aimed to create visual semblance of reality, the complex machinery of weights, counterweights, and traps camouflaged behind the proscenium. These conjured up such illusion on the stage that became indispensable to performance, and absolutely staple for the audience.

The Surabhi Company

The Surabhi Theatre Company was started in 1885 in the Cuddapah district of Andhra Pradesh by Vanarasa Govindarao and was named after his village, Surabhi.

Their first play it is believed was *Keechakavadha* from the Mahabharata which they presented in Surabhi itself. Though there were close on 46 groups with about 30 working actors each in the heyday of the company – and Surabhi remained enormously successful right till the 1960s and '70s – there is now only one single family with about 64 members upholding the tradition. The family, headed by R. Nageswara Rao, known also as Babji, lives about 40 kilometres away from the city of Hyderabad and often comes there to stage their plays. While they perform in built up auditoriums as well, the company also constructs its own theatre with corrugated tin sheets held together with ropes and wires. The construction takes a week to ten days.[12]

For most companies, including Surabhi, there is a set of stock curtains that migrate from performance

6. A still from the play *Chandipriya*, staged by Surabhi Theatre. Chandipriya prepares to go to Kashi in disguise.

to performance. Most companies do not get special curtains painted for each play, for two familiar reasons: as itinerant companies they have to travel light, and also because curtains, however closely they follow the rules of the rational construction of space, are never "actual locations but always a type of location, pristine romantic historical heroic"[13] and are "semiotically standardized"; where "natural settings often imply conjugality and romance, palace settings suggest status aspirations".[14]

The generalized backdrops of Parsi Theatre as also those of Surabhi include forest, garden, street, palace or durbar, *antahpur* (women's quarters), perhaps a cave scene (specially for Surabhi's enormously popular play *Mayabazar*), and sometimes heaven; curtains answering to current performances have more parks (for "love scenes") and streets with modern buildings.[15]

Rajadhyaksha and Willemen mention that in the era of Parsi Theatre, Haji Abdullah's *Sakhawat Khodadost Badshah,* staged by the Indian Imperial Company, used 14 curtains. The Zoroastrian Club's famous backdrop for *Badshah Ustaspa* showed the prophet Zarathustra with a ball of fire in his hands. The scenes painted became progressively more "real" or illusionistic and in Mama

7. A still from the play *Chandipriya*, staged by Surabhi Theatre. Raja Vasanta Rao's brother-in-law, who has overthrown the Raja, celebrates his victory.

8. A still from the play *Maha Bhagavata*, staged by Surabhi Theatre. Vishnu accompanied by his consort Lakshmi reclines on the serpent Shesha in Vaikuntha heaven. Brahma is shown seated on the lotus issuing from Vishnu's navel.

9. A still from the play *Maha Bhagavata*, staged by Surabhi Theatre. Devaki and Vasudeva, Krishna's parents, in conference.

Warerkar's *Satteche Gulam* (1922), the painter P.S. Kale used enlarged photographs as grids to duplicate Bombay streets on stage curtains.[16]

In order to paint the drop scene, tacker nails are used to stretch the cloth – *kora kapra* or marking cloth – on a frame that is kept standing on the ground. The painters work from top down, using bamboo ladders when needed. At first, they do a rough sketch with pencil or crayon to accommodate all that is essential for the specific backdrop. After this, "mother colour" (flat ground colour) is applied. Over this, outline and details are drawn. Finally, actual colour and highlights are added. Till about 100 years ago stone and mineral colours were used. These were powdered and mixed with gum Arabic and applied on the cloth. Over the last 75 years or so, oxide colours available in the market are mixed with linseed oil and turpentine. For cheaper work, oxide colours are mixed with gum Arabic, but for more lasting and therefore expensive work Fevicol is added to linseed oil and turpentine. Nowadays even acrylic colours are being used. The thick *kora kapra* is treated with a water-based solution of zinc oxide which is applied with a shoe-polish brush. Complicated lighting

on translucent cloth, often nylon, creates moons, mists, and vapour for romantic scenes.

Until about 25 years ago the company had resident scene painters, an occupation that was for the most part dynastic; they painted new curtains as well as undertook repair work. It was usual to have a resident tailor as well who continued with the company for generations. Today, Surabhi and other companies get work done by specific artists on an ad hoc basis, which they call piece work.[17]

Mise en scène or the gallery of pictures

The performance of the Surabhi Company proceeds as it were by means of a gallery of pictures; and the cargo of meaning, and of pleasure, proceeds in a series as well. An "anthological"[18] experience, that is, of pleasure based on a *collection* of sensations and not on their *advancement,* these curtains, as expected, are not painted on an escalating scale of beauty; quite the opposite, in fact, of the dramatic narrative which ascends rapidly towards its denouement. In the curtains there is no "maturation", to use a phrase of Barthes' again,[19] and as they are not incremental you are not

10. A still from the play *Maha Bhagavata*, staged by Surabhi Theatre. Narada meets Kamsa.

obliged to wait for the next one to understand the import of the play. For that reason no image is insipid, and none is surplus; indeed there may be an *excess* of pictorialization, and of opulence for the spectator's enjoyment.

The curtains typically manifest locations analogous to the ones summoned through dialogue and song, and therefore interpolate the performers into physically defined, almost material space wherein tableaux, which are the consequence of these locations, might be composed; but they also provide a spectacular and fantastic space beyond the illusionistic one. So on the one hand, the narrative is *grounded* by the atmosphere produced by the curtains; on the other, paradoxically, the world of romance and dream is *released,* indeed made practicable, only through their presence.

The "magnetic power" of the framed segment[20] produces what Elin Diamond, in the context of the

Restoration stage, calls a "spectator fetishist",[21] a description which seems to me to be particularly apt when describing the effects of the pictorial illusionism of the Surabhi curtain, a spectator fetishist who desires and awaits the seductions of the curtains and the voluptuousness of the stage. What adds to the wonder of viewing this foundational technology is the fact that it is labour-intensive; carpenters, painters, lights men, makeup artists, stage hands pull, push, counterweight, hoist, ballast, and drop the curtain apparatus; all playing a part in producing a fleeting, illusory, and often breathtakingly self-regarding stage picture.

Having receded behind the picture-frame stage and therefore becoming unquestionably a part of the picture that the stage is framing, the actor appears to have either *retreated* into the picture, which like the actor also calls equally for attention, or appears to have been *pressed up* from it in low relief. Lit by a bank of floodlights hanging just below the proscenium

11. A still from the play *Maha Bhagavata*, staged by Surabhi Theatre. Yashoda, Krishna's foster mother, listens to complaints about Krishna from the women of the vicinity.

12. A still from the play *Maha Bhagavata*, staged by Surabhi Theatre. Krishna embraces his mother Yashoda.

(among other lights), the curtains have no shadowed areas except those that have been painted in, and the actors too are just as brightly illumined; because of the frontal light bank they too have very little moulding by shadow, very little by way of chiaroscuro. Indeed many of the Surabhi curtains are so highlighted that they appear to give off light as if gilded, with colour serving as light.[22] Brilliantly costumed actors, set against a sumptuous backdrop, give the impression of being governed, as it were, by an aesthetic of effulgence.

The mise en scene then rests somewhere between the frieze and the tableau; like a frieze it creates a large, bold reproduction of environment with, for instance, substantial pillars and sinuous undulating curtains, or overabundant trees with a highly coloured trellis of leaves – a self-contained world; but like a tableau, a world which looks outwards and is therefore in some senses contingent on the viewer.

If the tableau is a pure *segment* that *contains* meaning – made precise by positioning and deportment – within its magnetized edges, meaning which is outside the sequentiality of the narrative, and which

is discharged towards the audience; the frieze appears to have several currents that recede and advance, spin and slant. If for the moment I translate the frieze into a theatrical mise en scene, I might suggest that it engages the viewer in a radically different way than the tableau. In the frieze there are different angles of address and engagement, diverse asides and monologues that do not yield a particular idea; placed in this plural environment that is both frieze and tableau, the Surabhi actor appears to allow allusions to circulate unevenly.

The genealogy of the Surabhi curtain assumes a lot of traffic among various popular art forms. India's modern popular imagery is a consequence of the cultural and technological adaptations of the 19th century. These include the pedagogy of the colonial art school that put value on perspective; mass production of images; acquaintance with European pictures circulating in the Indian market; the arrival of the techniques of engraving, lithography, and oleography; the development of photography and later of cinema, technologies that presented an exceptional experience to the viewer – of encountering a differently graded sensuous landscape and an almost tangible, individualized human figuration.[23] The theatre backdrops would have adapted and rendered what the painters understood as perspectival illusionism grasped from these various intersecting points. They might have demarcated background from foreground so that the actor's posture accommodated to the given circumstance of the background in the way that academic painting was doing; or in the way that Raja Ravi Varma (1848–1906) was contextualizing his historical/mythological/modern figures within his frame.

In the present day, viewers of Surabhi performances might come across, on a daily basis, billboards, advertisements, film posters from Bombay and from Tamil and Telugu cinema, they may watch a great deal of TV and TV soap, and of course cinema. This wide-ranging visual plurality may well migrate to the picture-frame stage that Surabhi constructs today. Thus the Surabhi stage appears to accommodate several different spaces within it; several sites that are in themselves, and within the chronology of time, even incompatible.[24] I mean for instance that the costume of the characters might install them within the fashion systems of Telugu cinema, while the depiction of a courtly space painted on the scene curtain may chart a course through the notions of majesty obtained from provincial Mughal schools of painting; the foliage or even a particular tree, gained from the Deccani miniatures. Flatly laid out clouds as well as stoutly painted pillars, even if they appear to do very different things, do not cancel each other out, rather they point to the intent of garnering all means at hand to captivate the viewer. The Surabhi stage, then, brings to mind, several evocations: a popular oleograph, for instance; or the considered staging of Ravi Varma; or the vigour of the Kuchipudi performance.[25]

It seems to me that, for someone like myself, who has followed the work of Surabhi for many years, it is the *surplus of illusion* in the performance that is compelling. The Surabhi stage creates a space of fantasy far in excess of the illusionist space that all theatres in any case create. It is a "floating" space,[26] meticulously and affectionately assembled, a *"place without a place"*, entirely illusory, that yet contains a performance

enacted at once, simultaneously, in *several* time zones. It is a performance that is "closed in on itself" but is at the same time given over to the audience, so as to permit a viewing of its special treasures that are collected from diverse eras, styles, and grammars of theatre, visuality, and architectural convention; from folk traditions, painted scrolls, photographic backdrops, and cinema, audaciously modified and laid out for its present consumers.

FIGURE ACKNOWLEDGEMENTS

Figures 1–7 by S. Thyagarajan, National School of Drama, New Delhi; figures 8–12 by P. Sripathi, Hyderabad.

NOTES

[1] Richard Southern, *Changeable Scenery,* London: Faber and Faber, 1952, pp. 164–65.

[2] Ibid., p. 165.

[3] Ibid., p. 165.

[4] Ibid., p. 164.

[5] Kathryn Hansen, "Parsi Theatre and the City: Locations, patrons, audiences", *Sarai Reader 2002: The Cities of Everyday Life,* pp. 40–49, see p. 44. The description is more like that of an Act Drop than a Drop Scene.

[6] *Changeable Scenery*, pp. 32–33.

[7] Ibid., p. 167.

[8] See, among others, *Changeable Scenery.*

[9] Michael R. Booth, *Theatre in the Victorian Age,* Cambridge: Cambridge University Press, 1991, p. 71.

[10] The Parsi Theatre which is usually understood to have had its heyday between the 1850s and the 1930s, was, as the name suggests, subsidized in great measure by the Parsis, Zoroastrians of Persian origin who had settled on India's western coast. The Bombay Theatre, built in 1776 as a copy of London's Drury Lane, was bought up in 1835 by a Parsi, Sir Jamsetjee Jejeebhoy. By the 1890s, Parsi Companies employed full time writers and troupes of salaried actors, built their own theatres, and also began publishing their plays. The Companies could have Parsi financiers, patrons, actor-managers, or actors, but they were by no means exclusively Parsi. There was a lot of cross-region and even cross-language movement of artists, writers, and performers. Although the Parsi Theatre survived till the 1940s, a large number of Theatre Companies transformed into cinema studios in the 1920s after the Indian cinema industry was inaugurated in 1913. The performance protocol of the

Parsi Theatre was hybridized. The Parsi Theatre drew on the singing and performing traditions of 19th-century Indian courtesans, including forms like ghazal, thumri, dadra, hori. It drew on Victorian melodrama and its complex stage machinery, on Shakespeare as enacted by Western touring companies, European realistic narrative structures, British amateur theatricals, pageants and local forms, as also on the visual regime of the celebrated Indian painter Raja Ravi Varma (1848–1906). This mix was enormously successful in the subcontinent and beyond, and may be seen as India's first truly profitable modern commercial theatre. For more details, see my "Parsi Theatre" in Ananda Lal (ed.), *The Oxford Companion to Indian Theatre*, New Delhi: Oxford University Press, 2004. See also Somnath Gupta, *Parsi Thiyetar: Udhbahav aur Vikas*, Illahabad: Lokbharati Prakashan, 1981; Lakshmi Narayan Lal, *Parsi-Hindi Rangmanch*, Delhi: Rajpal and Sons, 1973; Ranvir Singh (ed.), *Parsi Thiyetar*, Jodhpur: Rajasthan Sangit Natak Akademi, 1990.

[11] Elin Diamond, *Unmaking Mimesis*, London and New York: Routledge, 1997, p. 58.

[12] See among others http://www.the hindu.com/2006/01/20/stories/2006012012880300.htm for references to Surabhi.

[13] Arjun Appadurai's formulation while referring to backdrops; Arjun Appadurai, "The Colonial Backdrop", *Afterimage*, 24: 5 (March/April 1997), pp. 4–7.

[14] Ibid.

[15] Personal communication, Jyotindra Jain.

[16] Ashish Rajadhyaksha and Paul Willemen (eds.), *Encyclopedia of Indian Cinema*, Delhi: Oxford University Press, 1995.

[17] I am grateful to Jyotindra Jain for providing me with this detail.

[18] Roland Barthes, *Image–Music–Text*, Glasgow: Fontana, 1977, p. 72.

[19] Ibid.

[20] Ibid., pp. 70–72.

[21] *Unmaking Mimesis*, p. 59.

[22] I am grateful to Geeta Kapur for drawing my attention to this.

[23] See Jyotindra Jain, "Morphing Identities: Reconfirming the Divine and the Political" in Indira Chandrasekhar and Peter Seel (eds.), *Body.City: Siting contemporary culture in India*, Berlin: House of World Cultures and Delhi: Tulika Books, 2003, pp. 12–46.

[24] See for instance Michel Foucault, "Of Other Spaces", *Diacritics* 16 (Spring 1986), pp. 22–27 on heterotopias; I am grateful to Jyotindra Jain for bringing my attention to these ideas.

[25] I am grateful to Nilima Sheikh for pointing out these possibilities to me.

[26] Michel Foucault, "Of Other Spaces", while referring to a boat, p. 27.

ADDITIONAL REFERENCES

Michael R. Booth, Richard Southern, Frederick and Lise-Lone Marker, Robertson Davies, *The Revels History of Drama in English*, Vol. VI 1770–1880, London: Methuen, 1975.

Tapati Guha-Thakurta, *The Making of a New "Indian" Art: Artists, Aesthetics and Nationalism in Bengal, c. 1850–1920*, Cambridge: Cambridge University Press, 1998.

Vidyavati Lakhmanrav Namra, *Hindi Rangmanch aur Pandit Narayan Prasad Betab*, Varanasi: Vishvavidyalaya Prakashan, 1972.

Christopher Pinney, *Photos of the Gods*, Delhi: Oxford University Press, 2004.

DE
constructing the nation

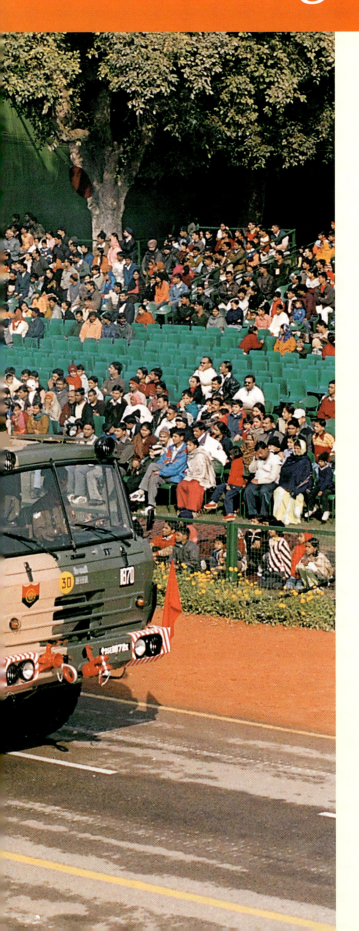

Jyotindra Jain

Among the various mechanisms of cultural activation aimed at strategizing ideological control in India, the role of image mobilization – of symbols, icons, performatives, and spectacles – as evident in India's Republic Day Parade has been scarcely analysed. Under the rubric of nation, performance, and representation, I shall examine the Republic Day Parade organized every January 26, since 1950, by the Government of India to celebrate the anniversary of India becoming a Democratic Republic in that year.

The Parade is primarily a military affair in which the Defence services bravery awards are presented by the President of India and the latest tanks, missiles, radar systems, air force planes, defence communications systems, etc., mounted on trucks, are paraded, followed by marching contingents of army, navy, and air force bands (figure 1). After the Indo-Pakistan conflict in Kargil in 2000, a tableau showing India's victory over Pakistan was paraded amidst much cheer from the audience. For the powerful military hardware of Western technological origin to not hurt national pride, a genealogical connection to "traditional" technology of war in the historical past, beyond effective historical continuity, had to be invented.[1] In the Parades of 1967 and 1969 fictional regiments of soldiers from "Seven Dynastic Periods" of Indian history, ranging from the 7th to the 18th century were re-enacted. The costumes consisted of an imaginary attire comprising elements of hairstyle and headgear, clothing, caps, and weapons, randomly selected from the archives of sculpture, painting, or literary descriptions of respective ages or from the generalized memory of history and tradition (figures 2–4). Here, by juxtaposing a historicist reconstruction of visual stereotypes (evoking age-old exotic fantasies of a past Golden Age) with imported

1. (*previous pages*) State-of-the-art missiles on display, Republic Day Parade, 2002. Photograph: Mela Ram, New Delhi.

2. Fictional regiment of the Chalukya dynasty, Republic Day Parade, 1967. Photograph: Photo Division, D.P.R., Ministry of Defence, Government of India.

3. Fictional regiment of
the "Sultanate period",
Republic Day Parade, 1967.
Photograph: Photo Division,
D.P.R., Ministry of Defence,
Government of India.

4. Fictional regiment of
the "Rajput period" (front),
Republic Day Parade, 1967.
Photograph: Photo Division,
D.P.R., Ministry of Defence,
Government of India.

modern weaponry, the nation is projected as an unruptured, homogeneous entity with the past and the present merging seamlessly.[2]

The military display is followed by a cultural pageant comprising tableaux and dioramas depicting the achievements of different ministries and departments of the state governments and the Government of India,[3] as well as those of folk culture and dances representing the states of the Indian Union (figures 5–7). The event is watched live by an estimated 200,000 viewers and by millions on television.

The spectacle is held at Rajpath (a literal translation of its colonial name, Kingsway), a neo-classical imperial axis of Lutyens' Delhi, modelled after the Champs-Elysees in Paris with its three architectural points, i.e. the Palace of Louvre (Rashtrapati Bhavan in Delhi), the Egyptian Obelisk (Jaipur column), and the Arc de Triomphe (India Gate).

On Republic Day, the imperial axis is emblematized as the space of the Indian nation itself, with the President, Prime Minister, Defence Minister, and the heads of the three Defence services, among others,

5. Tableau representing Meghalaya, emphasizing the "children of nature" syndrome, Republic Day Parade, 2006. Photograph: Photo Division, D.P.R., Ministry of Defence, Government of India.

present on the site. They represent the Indian Union, and occupy the central rostrum, which is surrounded by stands of seats for spectators hierarchized in descending order from the political supremos and diplomats, to the common people. The Union watches its states being paraded down below, their identities condensed into cultural tableaux or dioramas mounted on camouflaged tractors propagating unity in diversity. The nation thus staged is consecrated by the chants of the national anthem and patriotic songs.

In the years between 1946, when India's Constituent Assembly was elected, and 1950, when India adopted the Republican Constitution, it had become clear that its political predicament and the problems related to its cultural and ideological diversity were posing a threat to its ambition of long-term integration as one harmonious country.[4] From the pressures arising out of the assertion of ethnic and religious identities to cries of religious nationalism and regionalist movements based on linguistic, communal, and ethnic criteria, India's national integration was threatened.

At this juncture Prime Minister Nehru repeatedly

6. Tableau representing Karnataka, displaying the Mysore Palace and the royal elephant, Republic Day Parade, 2006. Photograph: Photo Division, D.P.R., Ministry of Defence, Government of India.

spoke of India's cultural unity and opposed the idea of redrawing the map of India based on ethnic or linguistic divides. For Nehru the "glory of India has been the way in which it has managed to keep two things going at the same time: that is, its infinite variety and at the same time its unity in that variety".[5] Besides the strong constitutional and administrative strategies to sustain territorial integrity, the need arose to evolve a whole range of visual symbols, performances, and spectacles, providing a unifying effect on separatist elements. Besides the national anthem, patriotic songs, and the national calendar, a range of visual symbols such as the national flag, the national emblem, the national flower, the national bird, and the national animal were identified, imaged, even totemized.[6] Most of these symbols constituted the iconography of Bharat

7. Tableau representing Gujarat, underlining its ethnic culture, Republic Day Parade, 2006. Photograph: Photo Division, D.P.R., Ministry of Defence, Government of India.

7. Tableau representing Gujarat, underlining its ethnic culture, Republic Day Parade, 2006. Photograph: Photo Division, D.P.R., Ministry of Defence, Government of India.

Mata or Mother India – the map of India conceived as a sari-clad mother goddess.

Despite Nehru's apprehension, several compulsions within the Congress Party and outside eventually led to the gradual division of India into 28 states from 1952 to 2000 – some using the linguistic ploy and others imaginary ethnic identity as criteria. The Republic Day cultural pageant, which primarily comprises tableaux and dioramas representing the ethnic identities of the states condensed as cultural icons, was given aesthetic and ideological shape by Nehru himself. This basic shell of the pageant remains functional till date as the notion of Indian cultural nationalism appeals to almost all political parties, providing ample scope for representation of ideological and political concerns.

Jacques Derrida said: "The archivization produces as much as it records the event."[7] In this article, I shall analyse the Republic Day Parade and Pageant, historically and structurally, to show how the identity of communities (and, by extension, of the nation) and their cultural performances were systematically reconstructed and consciously restored in the framework of the Parade. Indeed, archivization does produce an event, but the process involves a complex and strategic transformation from stillness to motion, from abstract idea to action.

The archive is by nature static, fixed, abstract, and inscriptive. Performance, on the other hand, relies on live presences and is ephemeral, embodied. In this sense, the cultural tableaux and the folk dance festival that form important constituents of the Republic Day Parade could be called a "performed archive", wherein performance fertilizes the archive and vice versa. But by performing/mobilizing the abstract idea (represented by the static archive), the Parade legitimizes and thereby enacts a certain image of the nation – "materialized identity accomplished through the performativity of movement".[8] The association of the term "mobilization", especially with regard to identities, with political rallies and parades, is not casual. Both political activities and performance are kinaesthetic practices that require the mobilized body. Nehru's idea of "unity in diversity" was a concept – recorded in stillness on paper – that

awaited mobilization. With that, his shaping of the Republic Day Parade became "the practical dynamic between production and product",[9] that is to say between aptitude for action and corporealized identity. This notion of the power of a mobilized idea or ideology appealed to Nehru immensely and led him to properly institutionalize the Republic Day Parade in 1952, having as its major components a cultural pageant comprising tableaux of folk and tribal life of each state and a Folk Dance Festival (figures 8 and 9). Nehru writes:

> Thus the procession would be a moving pageant of India in its rich diversity. ... I would love to see in our procession people from various parts of India including our tribal people, the Nagas from the North East, the Bhils from Central India, the Santals and others showing that they are also full partners in this great enterprise of India going ahead.[10]

It is striking that the three key phrases in the above excerpt – "procession", "moving pageant", and "India going ahead" – literally refer to motion and by implication to mobilization, i.e. the "mobilization of participation"[11] of the people in the notion of unity in diversity and "in this great enterprise of India going ahead".

The cultural tableaux and dances were strategically reshaped, and sometimes even invented. "Culture" emerged as effect and though its immediate site of production was the Parade, eventually it began to "heal into its presumptive past and its present

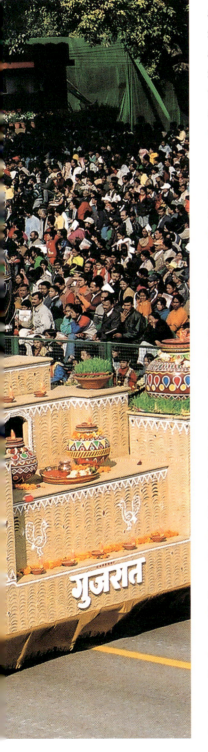

8. (*right*) Prime Minister Nehru amidst Chamba dancers, participants in the Folk Dance Festival, Republic Day celebrations, New Delhi, 1954. Photograph: Sangeet Natak Akademi, New Delhi.

9. Kabui Naga dance by Nrityasrama Troupe, Manipur, Republic Day celebrations, New Delhi, 1954. Photograph: Sangeet Natak Akademi, New Delhi.

cultural context like well-set bone. ...judgements about authenticity hard to make".[12]

These visual archives of restored images and performances have not only fed into their growth over 55 years but significantly begun to provide the standard for authentic cultural behaviour, self-image formation, and construction of identity back in the village and the tribe. The imitation of the reconstructed image of the self as projected by the nation at the Parade is absorbed into the community's self-identification back home – a kind of "projection" of the self "backward in time".[13]

Notably, the Government of India's guidelines issued to the states for submission of proposals for tableaux place a particular emphasis on *tradition, genuineness,* and *authenticity*:

In case of tableaux on cultural, historical/ traditional themes, the colours, designs, costumes, materials, etc. used should be *authentic.*

... It should be assured that the selected dance is a *genuine* folk dance and the costumes and musical instruments are *traditional* and *authentic.*

The "People of India" tableaux in the Parade, even today, are partially descendants of colonial anthropological archives, registers of orientalist photography, and the colonial museum dioramas, now reassembled to dream up a self-image for a nation vying for political and cultural solidarity. The cultural tableaux generally comprise highly romanticized depictions of what are construed to be important landmarks in Indian history; essentialized representations of tribal and village communities, "traditional" handicrafts, religious or domestic rituals, village markets, or peculiarities of regional landscapes (figures 10–13).

The tribals and villagers of these tableaux and dioramas appear to mimic their own restored self-images, as if living in a frozen space isolating themselves from any "evolving processes" and traces of "conflict and change".[14] The archived tribals of these peep-shows are devoid of wrist-watches, electrical poles, or cinema billboards, as the nation's measure of cultural authenticity is the distance in time and space, the distance from here and now.

With their exotic costumes or bare chests, their quaint-looking yet evocative dances, their "children of nature" image, the Parade tribals are proudly presented

10. Tableau representing Chhattisgarh, showing tribal ornaments, preceded by folk dancers and musicians of the state, Republic Day Parade, 2006. Photograph: Photo Division, D.P.R., Ministry of Defence, Government of India.

as living examples of India's ancient roots. These communities are staged by the state as "timeless" precisely because they are construed to be Adivasi, "original inhabitants", or autochthonous populations of the land and therefore "authentic". In fact, it has been customary to officially present "Tribal Chiefs" among the dignitaries invited to watch the Parade. These "Chiefs", who are quite randomly chosen to come and attend the event, are expected to wear their imaginary "traditional" attire (figure 14). For the audience watching the Parade, this aspect entails experiencing complex mechanisms of simultaneously engaging memory and selectively reimagining the present. As Joseph Roach has aptly put it, "...any performance of memory also enacts forgetting".[15] The state – as the spokesperson of India's ancient past, its culturally-conscious and modern present, as well as its promised bright future – uses the Parade tribals on two levels: firstly they represent pre-colonial history (by claiming them as India's "original" peoples), thereby appealing to the collective memory of the audience; secondly, to establish historical continuity by showing them performing live and also as spectators, in the same costumes as they might have been wearing centuries ago.

11. Tableau representing Karnataka, depicting the 12-yearly anointing of the Jain statue of Bahubali at Sravanabelgola, Republic Day Parade, 2005. Photograph: Photo Division, D.P.R., Ministry of Defence, Government of India.

12. Tableau representing Tamil Nadu, emphasizing the Hindu chariot festival, Republic Day Parade, 2006. Photograph: Photo Division, D.P.R., Ministry of Defence, Government of India.

13. Tableau representing Orissa, highlighting the appliqué craft of Pipli, Republic Day Parade, 2006. Photograph: Photo Division, D.P.R., Ministry of Defence, Government of India.

As such, the incorporation of the Parade tribals forms a part of the larger scheme to establish an essentialist image of India – essentialized through that very state-sanctioned "diversity". The cultural tableaux primarily serve the purpose of annually reiterating an official notion of "Indian-ness", a necessarily exclusionist idea.

Through exposure to sights that are far removed for the majority of the Parade audience – both geographically and temporally – it experiences defamiliarization on two levels. For one, the Parade audience in Delhi and TV audiences across the country would perceive all floats, even those from their own states, as exotic because the performances presented on the floats are transferred from their native regions and adapted (through excessive costume, accessories, gesture, condensement, etc.) to fit the occasion. For a spectator from Tamil Nadu, the float from Nagaland might seem "exotic" by virtue of the two places being culturally so far apart, but even the Nagas[16] themselves might feel proud and at the same time estranged, because in the wake of cultural change and influence of Christianity, they might no longer engage in "traditional" Naga practices, or be aware of what these practices entailed. Through this ostensibly paradoxical interplay of taking pride in and alienation from the idea of India, the nation ultimately affirms itself through its overall motto of unity in diversity. The message conveyed is that it is perfectly acceptable to feel unfamiliar; after all India's diversity could never be grasped by any single group. The Parade legitimizes itself by offering one the possibility to be acquainted with its richness and thereby to strengthen one's national identity. The second level of defamiliarization that the Parade generates is through its reference to an ancient historical past, which can be traced back to an imaginary "Golden Age" and which leads us right up to the India of today, thereby establishing a sense of historical continuity of the Indian nation. The histories and myths of origin that are presented as part of this "Golden Age" alienate the audience by the sheer force of their temporal distance. The events that are depicted (King Ashoka's remorse after the Kalinga War, King Harshavardhana distributing wealth in the presence of Xuanzang, the fortitude of the Rani of Jhansi, Tipu

14. "Tribal Chiefs" in the audience at the Republic Day Parade, 1969. Photograph: Photo Division, D.P.R., Ministry of Defence, Government of India.

Sultan's battle against the British, or the re-enactment of fictional regiments from seven dynastic periods of Indian history, mentioned earlier), establish a sense of historical continuity, which, though exoticizing the past, nonetheless reassert the force of Indian identity today. This interplay of "uncanny otherness" and "uncanny familiarity"[17] becomes the Parade's main thrust and powerfully reiterates Nehru's emblematic dictum of "unity in diversity".

Usually, the culture bureaucrats of the Central and state governments and often the experts hired by them to conceptualize and design the tableaux and organize folk dance groups had little direct knowledge about specific folk cultures and dances except for the fact that the official guidelines required them to concern themselves with "tradition" and "authenticity". These experts were busy inventing tradition to adapt and adjust to the aesthetic and practical requirements of the event in Delhi. For them often "tradition" and "authenticity" were abstracted, generalized national categories which in the context of folk culture often found expression in such cliches as "riotous colours", "full-throated singing", "infectious rhythm", "gay abandon", "raw energy", "cultures unaffected by the evils of civilization", etc.

Whenever there was a shortfall in the knowledge about a specific regional cultural tradition or a need for adaptation for aesthetic or practical considerations, the regional tradition was altered by "con-fusing" local traditional elements with those of a generalized Indian tradition. In fact the seamless osmosis of the specifically local and the generalized national is not considered to be an unwelcome byproduct in serving the objective of national integration. The archives of this generalized Indian cultural tradition are rich and users are least concerned about any knowledge of specificities of time, space, and context which, as is pointed out by John Pemberton in the context of Indonesia's national rituals in President Suharto's time, "has the effect, then, of motivating an almost endless production of offerings, a constant rearticulation of things cultural, in an attempt to make up for what may have been left out in the process of recovering 'tradition'. Or, tradisi [tradition] itself has emerged as a kind of meta-spook endowed with a profound appetite that virtually guarantees the reproduction of devotedly cultural desires, that is, the desire for culture."[18]

The basic objective behind presenting recovered tradition is that of "performing the nation" in its cultural diversity while attempting to integrate it with the thread of abstracted, generalized notions of Indian tradition. By strategically merging the local or the diverse with the national or the abstracted generalized Indian/national tradition, a spectacle is staged on Republic Day which generates an archive of images. Proliferated through the media, it produces not only the event, but restored identities of people and thereby of the nation.

Govind Vidyarthi, who was technical officer in the 1950s and '60s at the Sangeet Natak Akademi and in that capacity was "intimately connected with the Republic Day Folk Dance Festival from its very inception",[19] records revealing incidents of the process by which generalized "Indian" folk and tribal tradition were restored and enacted.

With more and more urban people presenting folk dances there has been an increasing tendency to include pretty college girls and even "extras" who dance for the films. Usually a Dance-Director-Choreographer accompanies

them and one could see in the Talkatora Camp hectic rehearsals for the "creation" of a folk dance. These urban folk dancers are a feast for the camera and they hit the headlines in the press.[20]

The State governments allot money for buying new dresses for the dance parties going to Delhi. The officials with no grasp or respect for traditions provide them with costumes made of what they consider attractive colours. A few years back a party of tribal men were brought from Vindhya Pradesh in full-sleeve shirts of yellow, red, blue, and white satin. Only two years back a group of Riang tribal girls from Tripura were seen draped in full-sleeve satin blouses.[21]

According to an officer of the Sangeet Natak Akademi, the dresses were carefully folded up and preserved for one of the subsequent festivals. By intense repetition, a community acquires a new visual identity, a mark of recognition of their "tradition" and since these "created" urban folk dances become a feast for the camera and hit the headlines in the press, their new identity gets documented and archived as *their* tradition (figure 15).

The generalized tradition operates as a sort of loose and shifting conglomerate of arbitrary cultural motifs suffused with symbolic values which may, through repeated performance, "attempt to establish continuity with a suitable historic past" or a distant regional cultural practice. Such a generalized tradition played a decisive role in simulating a bond between the diverse regional culture and the idealized Indian tradition.

The Republic Day Folk Dance Festival eventually formed the basis for canonization of Indian folk and tribal dance practices and was even seen as "an intense experience of the multiple traditions in their totality."[22] Dance historians[23] repeatedly used images from this Festival to illustrate their books on Indian folk dances. Several photographers built archives of these images and published them as examples of India's folk and tribal dance and culture.

15. Uniformly dressed-up
folk/tribal dancers at the
Republic Day Parade, 1969.
Photograph: Photo Division,
D.P.R., Ministry of Defence,
Government of India.

This objectified visual identity – through its multiple quotes and citations, in print and electronic media, philately, tourism, museums, maps, Festivals of India, etc. – became a powerful tool for imaging India's specific cultural identity and for national integration of a culturally diverse society.

NOTES

[1] Eric Hobsbawm and Terence Ranger (eds.), *The Invention of Tradition*, Cambridge, 1983, p. 7.

[2] See Christophe Jaffrelot, *The Hindu Nationalist Movement in India*, New York, 1996, p. 13: "Subsequently, their main concern was to endow that renewed tradition with the sanction of...the challenge of the West."

[3] For example, some of the tableaux between the 1950s and '70s included, "Wheels of Progress", "Wheat for the Nation", "Employment, Food and Nourishment for the Poor". Significantly, the tableaux between the 1980s and 2006 pertained to atomic energy, telecommunications, and the Delhi Metro.

[4] The main political problems at this time included the strife between the Muslim League and the Constituent Assembly, the reality of the Partition of India, and the relations of the country with the princely states.

[5] Speech in the Constituent Assembly, November 8, 1948, *Jawaharlal Nehru's Speeches*, vol. 1, New Delhi: Publications Division, reprint 1963, p. 41. In this context, also see Jim Masselos, "India's Republic Day: The Other 26 January", in *South Asia*, Vol. XIX, special issue (1996), pp. 183–203, and Srirupa Roy, "Instituting Diversity. Official Nationalism in Post-independence India", in *South Asia*, Vol. XXII, No. 1 (1999), pp. 79–99.

[6] The national emblem is the lion capital of an Ashokan column; the national flower is the lotus; the national bird is the peacock; and the national animal is the tiger.

[7] Jacques Derrida, *Archive Fever: A Freudian Impression*, trans. Eric Prenowitz, Chicago and London, 1995, p. 17.

[8] Randy Martin, *Critical Moves: Dance Studies in Theory and Politics*, Durham and London, 1998, p. 4.

[9] Ibid.

[10] Nehru's letter dated September 10, 1952, addressed to the Chief Ministers of the States, Ministry of Education, file no. 6-11/52-G, 2(A), in National Archives, New Delhi.

[11] Martin, *Critical Moves*, p. 4.

[12] Richard Schechner, *Performative Circumstances: From the Avant Garde to Ramlila*, Calcutta, 1983, p. 184.

[13] Ibid., p. 186.

[14] Both quotes from James Clifford, "Four Northwest Coast Museums: Travel Reflections", in Ivan Karp and Steven B. Lavine (eds.), *Exhibiting Cultures: The Poetics and Politics of Museum Display*, Washington, 1991, p. 215 and p. 218 respectively.

[15] Joseph Roach, *Cities of the Dead: Circum-Atlantic Performance*, New York, 1996, p. 122.

[16] The name "Naga" stands for a generalized ethnic group comprising several varying tribes bunched together by the colonial Census as one community.

[17] Roach, *Cities of the Dead*, p. 148.

[18] John Pemberton, *On the subject of "Java"*, Ithaca and London, 1994, p. 11.

[19] Govind Vidyarthi, "Republic Day Folk Dance Festival", *Sangeet Natak* (Journal of the Sangeet Natak Akademi, New Delhi), April–June 1969, p. 84.

[20] Ibid., p. 82.

[21] Ibid.

[22] Chandralekha, review of Kapila Vatsyayan, *Traditions of Indian Folk Dances*, New Delhi, 1974, in *The Times of India*, August 28, 1976.

[23] Vatsyayan, *Traditions...*, and Mohan Khokar, *Splendour of Indian Dance*, Himalayan Books, New Delhi, 1985.

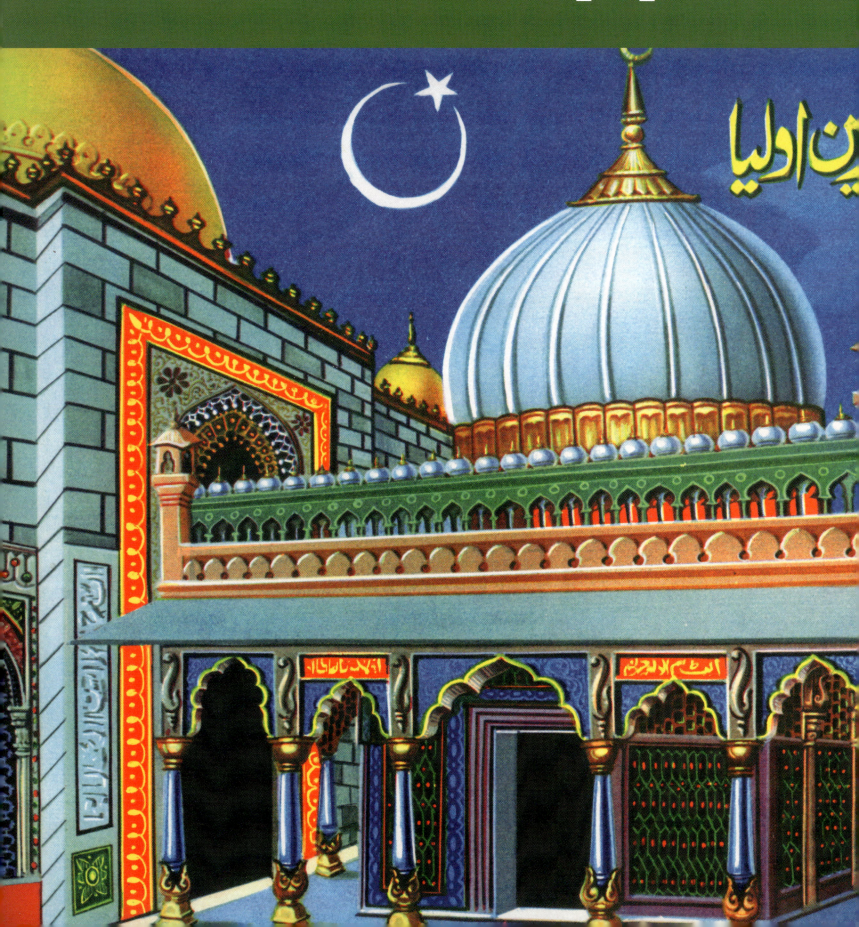

MECCA VERSUS THE LOCAL

orientation in the popular rel

SHRINE the dilemma of
igious art of Indian Muslims

Yousuf Saeed

Islam is often seen as a religion without any symbols or icons depicting God. But in practice, millions of Muslim believers, especially in South Asia, use a variety of popular devotional images. The popular calendar art of the Muslims sold on the streets of many Indian towns depicts not only images of Mecca and Medina, but also many shrines of local saints, their miracles and folklore, often portrayed as graphically as the Hindu mythical scenes. More importantly, the artists and the industry that produces such artworks are not necessarily all Muslim – many are Hindus. Thus it is easy to see Hindu or even Christian symbols being adopted in the Muslim images.

Since a sizeable number of Indian Muslims are unable to travel to Mecca for Hajj, local shrines and folklore play an important role in their religious lives. Devotees from smaller towns embark on many lesser pilgrimages, covering in a trip many tombs of saints such as Nizamuddin Aulia at Delhi or Khwaja Moinuddin Chishti at Ajmer, especially during their Urs (death anniversary) celebrations, and need to take home some sacred souvenirs. What better gift than a religious poster that is bright and colourful, has devotional as well as decorative value, and helps them (and their folks at home) relate to the big shrine and its fervour? Many people buy posters at major festivals such as Id or Ramzan and use them to decorate a newly painted house or a shop (just as many Hindus do around Divali). Since a poster or calendar is meant to decorate the walls of a home, its imagery should not be morbid, repulsive, or unattractive, even if the subject demands it that way. Young women or children, if depicted, are shown as embodiments of perfect innocence and beauty. A generous dose of greenery, flowers, hills, waterfalls, and other scenic elements is always thrown in as the backdrop, even in the case of a desert story!

Thus popular Sufi shrines, personages of the saints, and their special attributes become favourite subjects of this art form. It is important to study how average Muslim users of these images connect with the icons of the local shrine in relation to the images of Mecca and Medina. Are there any needs of the devotee that are fulfilled by a local shrine, which an image of

Mecca probably cannot? One also needs to explore how South Asia's Muslim iconography has not only been legitimized in Islam, but also allowed to thrive in the form of an urban mass culture. The syncretic tendencies of these popular images reflect a larger pluralistic culture that was prevalent through much of South Asia's past.

Looking into the origins of when and how the Muslim images entered the realm of the popular printing industry, one predictably finds the earliest examples coming out of the famed Ravi Varma Press, as early as 1910.[1] Later on, many other publishers such as Hemchand Bhargava (Delhi), H. Ghulam Muhammad & Sons (Lahore), and now, Brijbasi (Delhi) and J.B. Khanna (Chennai), among others, have focused on Muslim themes, employing a number of famed artists such as H.R. Raja, Balkrishnan, Mohideen Husain, Swarup, B.M. Kamal, Kishore, Bhatia, and so on. However, one may be curious to know the origins of the image of the shrine at Mecca in the minds of believing Muslims, prior to the age of printing/mass production. There seem to be four broad routes through which such images may have been imported here: (1) miniature paintings and illuminated books from Central Asia coming with early travellers/conquerors, (2) lithographs of European origin brought by the British or the Portuguese,

2. A roadside stall selling popular posters at Darya Ganj, Delhi. Notice the hierarchy of the images – some of those on top being Muslim popular posters.

1. (*previous pages*) The shrine of Hazrat Nizamuddin Aulia at Delhi. Notice the absence of any human figure – probably to qualify this as an iconoclastic image. Artist unknown, Publisher: Brijbasi.

3. Titled *Burraq-un Nabi*, the image shows a flying steed on which the Prophet Muhammad made his ascent to heaven (*Me'raj*). The face of the creature, the crown on her head and other ornaments are typically south Indian. Images of Burraq draw some inspiration from the Hindu image of Kamadhenu. Artist: M.S.S., Publisher unknown.

(3) miscellaneous items such as prayer mats, carpets, cloth hangings, and other objects with such images, brought by Indian pilgrims returning from Hajj, and more importantly (4) the non-visual accounts, either written or oral, about the shape and colour of the sacred buildings and the material culture of Arabia told by travellers or pilgrims and passed down the generations to those who could not visit Mecca or had no access to its image.

Miniature paintings from Central Asia are less likely to be the source of popular imagination about Mecca since most of these were commissioned by the royal court and never made public. European lithographs of Islamic shrines, drawn mostly for the travel books published in Europe in the 17th–18th centuries, may not have made it to South Asia until the end of the 19th century.[2] But some Muslim posters published by the Ravi Varma Press show the influence of the European lithograph style. A 1920 image depicting the battleground of Karbala (Iraq), for instance, shows a large empty courtyard surrounded by a few European-looking buildings with domes! The influence

of these early images does not seem to have lasted very long in Muslim poster-makers. Hence, the major inspiration for Muslim images seems to be the objects and memories brought by Indian pilgrims returning from Mecca. In many Indian towns and villages, a Haji (pilgrim) returning from Mecca was, and still is, welcomed with great fanfare, with the exterior of the houses being decorated with colourful paintings of Mecca and Medina, Quranic inscriptions, and even moral commandments written in Urdu, Hindi, or other local languages. Often, one sees a picture of an airplane, a ship, or a train along with the image of Mecca, to depict the mode of transport the pilgrim took – thereby signifying the status of the pilgrim in the locality.

One needs to make a distinction here, between the images of Arabian shrines and those of local Indo-Muslim shrines and folklore. The more documentary images of Mecca may have arrived late (probably via photographs), but the images of local Muslim saints, their mausoleums, and miracles may have existed in South Asia from much earlier times – along with the

4. Bait-al Muqaddas or the holy shrine of Jerusalem depicted along with mythical symbols of heaven, hell, and the tombs of Moses and David, besides others. The sun's rays radiate from Mount Sinai in the background. Artist and Publisher unknown.

6. (*facing page, below*) Shrine and personage of Hazrat Baba Shaikh Farid at Pakpattan, Pakistan. The image portrays his unique form of meditation called *Namaz-e Ma'kus* which involved hanging upside down in a well for several days. Also depicted is his compassion for nature. Artist: Sarwar Khan, Publisher unknown (purchased in Lahore, May 2005).

traditions of Hindu mythology. Although the persona of a Muslim saint or prophet has always been taboo for artists, one does find many Indian posters in this genre. One such image shows an imaginary gathering of some popular saints of South Asia – Baba Farid, Khwaja Qutbuddin Bakhtiyar, Khwaja Moinuddin Chishti, Hazrat Ghausul Azam, Hazrat Bu Ali Sharif, and Hazrat Nizamuddin Aulia, in a sort of gallery of portraits. Usually, there seems to be one central portrait of a saint that becomes the inspiration for later images. But in order to imagine the facial features of a saint, the original artist may have depended upon accounts of the saint available in oral or written biographical narratives. Often, the miracles or special powers of a saint provide the necessary visual element or backdrop of a portrait and its ambience.

Some posters collected from Pakistan recently show a surprising element: an unhindered depiction

5. (*right*) Cover of a devotional music cassette featuring a popular biography of the saint Ghausul Azam. The image of the shrine depicted on the cover comes from poster art. Artist unknown, Publisher: T-Series.

of the personages of saints, something many Indian publishers may still be reluctant about. In many posters printed in Lahore, one can prominently see artists' imaginings of saints like Khwaja Moinuddin Chishti of Ajmer, Baba Farid of Pakpattan, and many others. A large poster found very commonly in Pakistani towns is a mega photo collage of almost all Muslim saints revered in South Asia, from Ghausul Azam of Baghdad to some 20th-century *sajjadeh nashin*s or keepers of Sufi shrines, represented by faces cut out from photographs and paintings, each with a number, referring to an Urdu index of names given in the same frame. Of course, one can easily find the portraits of the twelve Imams, of Hazrat Ali, and of many members of the Prophet's family, in a somewhat European photo-realism that may have been imported from Iran. Many such portraits, popular among the Shia community in India and Pakistan, look clearly different from the local artistic styles commonly used in mythic figures such as Burraq or Duldul.

An artist's quest for putting in as many attributes about a saint and his shrine as possible within a frame, using minimum effort, results in a pastiche where an arch and a dome come from separate faded photographs, the saint's person comes from an old painting, the trees and hills are cut out of a Swiss landscape, the lion from a wildlife magazine, and the *diya*s or lamps from a Hindu poster. Further additions are the pictures of Mecca and Medina, Arabic inscriptions, and a crescent and star that may have been painted by the artist to add some originality. However, another way to look at these pastiches would be to see the plurality or syncretism of faith where a devotee or the artist does not mind invoking different gods and deities or different visual cultures for the fulfilment of their daily needs and pleasures.

The keepers of the Sufi shrines too play an important role in the proliferation of the devotional images. Some of the recent pastiche posters collected in Pakistan feature cut-out photographs of living or recently expired Sufi saints or the *sajjadeh nashin* of the shrine, along with the image of the shrine building and some miraculous elements such as a lion or a tiger. A humble devotee visiting the shrine, especially if he/she

7. (*previous pages*) The art of pastiche goes to extreme limits where probably every single element of this poster of the Shah Jamal shrine at Lahore has been derived from different sources. Yet the portrayal of the saint's ecstasy in this dance posture is quite evocative. Artist: Sarwar Khan, Publisher unknown.

8. A modern pastiche showing the cutouts of living or recently expired *sajjadeh nashin*s (caretakers) of the shrine at Golra Sharif near Islamabad, Pakistan. Artist: Sarwar Khan, Publisher unknown (purchased in Islamabad, August 2005).

9. (*facing page*) The shrine of Moinuddin Chishti in Ajmer, overshadowed with the images of the shrines at Mecca, Medina (top middle), Baghdad (top left), and Jerusalem (top right). At the bottom are inscribed the names of the five members of the holy family: Muhammad, Ali, Fatima, Hasan, and Husain. Artist: H.R. Raja, Publisher: BAP.

manages to meet or "see" its chief Sufi, would continue to relate to that experience with the help of a poster that has the saint's image along with his ancestors. The most evocative of such examples was found in Golra Sharif, a Sufi shrine near Islamabad, where hundreds of devotees form a long queue to shake or kiss the hands of the main *sajjadeh nashin*, after which each visitor is given a colourful visiting card that has photos of the saint, the shrine, and some supplications for the devotee to remember. This visiting card is no different from the large posters of the same shrine available outside or elsewhere in Pakistan – the two together help keep the memory of the saint and shrine alive, as well as provide the much sought-after legitimacy of their lineage – not to mention the offerings that the devotees make at such shrines.

In a study conducted among the users of Muslim devotional posters in India,[3] many respondents seemed unclear and often confused about their attitude and the status to be given to these images besides thinking of them as decorative items, unlike a Hindu devotee who uses the image or idol of a deity for worship.

10. Portrait of the saint Waris Shah and his female companion and the shrine near Barabanki, Uttar Pradesh. Notice the talisman designs in the form of numerical figures on the top corners. Artist unknown, Publisher: Brijbasi.

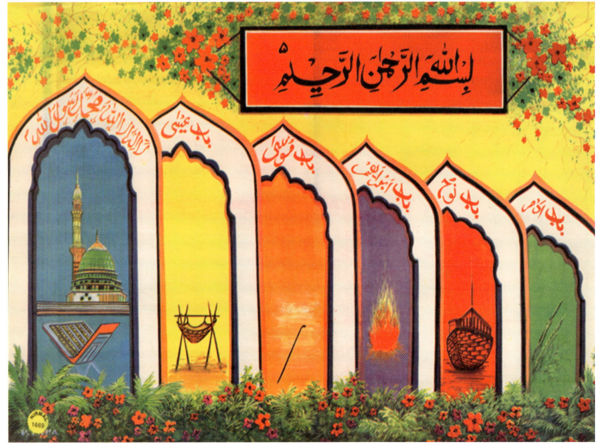

11. In a situation where the personages of biblical figures cannot be depicted, they are symbolized here in gates that show miracles associated with each prophet – Adam (extreme right) with stalks of wheat as forbidden fruit, Noah with the ark, Abraham with the fire, Moses with the staff, Jesus with a crib, and Muhammad with the green dome at Medina and the *Quran*. Artist unknown, Publisher: Nirmal.

Since most respondents came from poor or lower middle-class families or from rural areas, many were probably not familiar with the concept of iconoclasm in Islam. They broadly knew that idolatry is un-Islamic (this is what differentiates them from the Hindus), but the images of local saints, their tombs, other Islamic folklore, and many symbols of composite culture, ingrained in their collective/folk memory, are openly accepted and venerated, without drawing any lines between Islamic and un-Islamic – until someone with a *wahhabi* (purist) bent of mind intervenes in their practices.

So, what exactly goes on in the minds and hearts of the religious people who fall in the grey area between iconoclasm and idolatry? In theory, Islamic iconoclasm assumes that God is the sole author of life and anyone else producing the likeness of a living being seeks to rival God. Most devoted Muslims stay away from iconography due to a tradition (*hadith*) ascribed to the Prophet Muhammad that a person drawing the picture of a living thing would be asked on the Day

of Judgement to infuse life into it. But the *Quran*, interestingly, does not contain a single line prohibiting the drawing of representative figures – though it does taboo idolatry.

An obvious question to ask: if Islam prohibits iconic devotion, then what about the *Kaaba*, the cubical shrine at Mecca which every Muslim faces while praying, and the black stone embedded in it, which the pilgrims kiss? The *Kaaba*, the house of God (though the God doesn't live in it, according to the Muslims), was constructed by the Prophet Ibrahim (c. 2000 BCE), and has been visited by pilgrims ever since, who circumambulate it in a variety of rituals. The black stone, probably a meteorite, is the only relic left now from Ibrahim's shrine, and Prophet Muhammad is attributed to have kissed it, probably out of Semitic affinity. Pilgrims performing the *tawaf* or *parikrama* (circumambulation) of the *Kaaba* kiss or wave towards the black stone to mark each round. When the Prophet Muhammad re-entered Mecca in the 7th century CE and made his first Islamic pilgrimage (Hajj), he demolished most of the idols

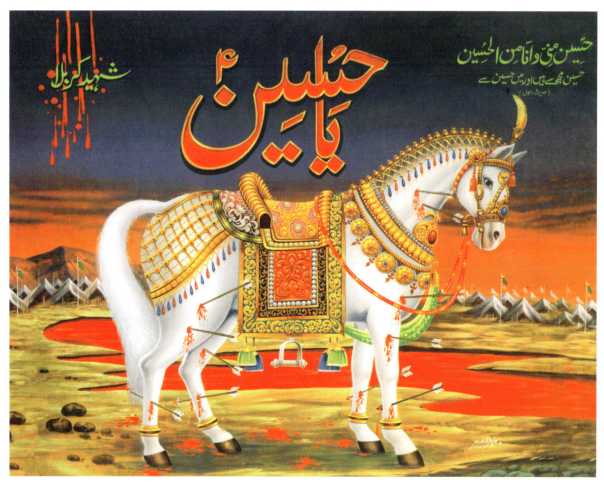

12. A scene from the Karbala war where Duldul, the horse of Imam Husain, is the only survivor standing amidst pools of blood. In other variants of this image, the backdrop has also been depicted pleasantly with flowers, greenery, and streams. Artist: H.R. Raja, Publisher unknown.

13. Part of a large map
showing details of the
structures in and around
the Ajmer shrine, especially
the two huge cauldrons
used to cook food for
the needy. Artist and
publisher unknown.

13. Part of a large map showing details of the structures in and around the Ajmer shrine, especially the two huge cauldrons used to cook food for the needy. Artist and publisher unknown.

therein, but retained some rituals of the pilgrimage that were reminiscent of the events from Ibrahim's life, probably for their importance in Arab society.

During the Prophet's life, the *Kaaba* was declared the *qibla* or pole to which Muslims turn for prayers, so that everyone always faces the same direction, rather than different ones – basically a gesture of monotheistic consolidation. Praying towards Mecca, in principle, does not mean worshipping the cubical shrine – it is there only to discipline and orient worshippers towards one God.[4] A pilgrim visiting the various sacred sites in and around Mecca is supposed to show only respect or homage (as shown to a historical monument) rather than adoration or veneration. But this is where the lines get blurred – an average pilgrim cannot differentiate between respect and veneration. Everyday, thousands of crying pilgrims want to touch and kiss the wall or the cloth cover of the *Kaaba*. But the Saudi authorities try to dissuade them, often forcefully, from doing so. In the graveyards in Mecca and Medina where some of the most significant personalities of early Islam are buried, there are no identifiable grave marks, to avoid their becoming the objects of adoration, as they do over much of South Asia or elsewhere.

However, the local multi-faith shrines, their rituals, and images in South Asia continue to invoke fervour among devotees. When all possible efforts fail to solve a particular problem in someone's life, she or he is ready to go to any extreme – any god, deity, priest, or house of worship that may resolve the crisis. People in distress often help each other with a little talisman, a *prasad* from Tirupati to cure a disease, or a *tawiz* from Nizamuddin Aulia to get the ideal job. The religious posters industry, which produces many colourful talismans too, keeps growing as long as the people's devotional needs get fulfilled. But interestingly, the orthodox Muslim clergy does not raise any objection to these graphic depictions, some of which in reality could be rather provocative to a purist Muslim's eye. Is it because these images circulate mostly among poor or rural Muslims, whose faith may be more pantheistic and icon-dependent, compared to their elite/urban brethren who follow a more iconoclastic and monotheistic faith? The role of the market certainly cannot be ignored in the propagation of this popular visual culture that keeps a multifarious Islam alive in South Asia.

NOTES

[1] Erwin Neumayer and Christine Schelberger, *Popular Indian Art, Raja Ravi Varma and the Printed Gods of India*, New Delhi: Oxford University Press, 2003.

[2] Desmond Stewart, *Early Islam*, New York: Time-Life Books, 1967.

[3] Yousuf Saeed, "Syncretism in the Popular Art of Muslim Religious Posters in North India", paper presented at the Centre for Studies in the Developing Societies, SARAI, New Delhi, August 2004.

[4] But isn't that what some Hindus and other icon-worshippers too believe – idols are not Gods themselves; they are only markers for concentration or *dhyana*.

THE BOMBAY FILM POSTER
a short biography

Ranjani Mazumdar

The film poster, created for the popularization and marketing of the moving image, has enjoyed a unique history ever since the birth of the cinema. Like the cinema, the poster has also gone through radical transformations linked to new technology, and the proliferation of visual culture in the 20th century. As in most parts of the world, film posters in India have historically formed an integral part of the distribution and circulation of films. These posters provide the viewer with a basic sense of the narrative through a frozen image whose form is derived from different traditions of popular, traditional, and modernist art cultures.[1] In this essay I will try to unravel the Indian film poster's cultural biography by posing a set of queries such as where and how and for whom the poster is produced, its relationship to technology, how it travels, who designs it, its lifespan, its typical cultural markers, how its value changes over time, and who owns the poster. These questions will inevitably take us into a complex maze of cultural, aesthetic, and social values that shape the way the poster functions as an object of art, an icon, a semiotic moment, and a commodity.[2]

It is difficult to give an exact date for the origin of the film poster. The first full-length feature made in India, *Raja Harishchandra* (Dadasaheb Phalke: 1913) was a mythological. Newspaper advertisements, handbills, and publicity booklets of the film can be traced, but no references to the use of posters have been found. The poster of the film *Kalyan Khajina* (Baburao Painter: 1924) is perhaps one of the earliest to have survived.[3] It was designed and painted by the director Baburao Painter himself. Posters were usually hand-painted on canvas and then used as the design source for printing on cheap paper. Since print was the most important medium of publicity, booklets of film songs and stories, handbills, and posters flourished in the studio era with the poster becoming the most significant and dominant form.[4]

Historically the poster has been important as a travelling form that moves from city walls to lavatories, from *pan* shops to huts. Used as a wall decoration in *dhaba*s and small hotels as well as to promote film culture, the poster is both an advertisement and a

cultural icon. Posters have circulated within urban centres for many years. Their presence outside cinema theatres and on city walls has been a prominent visual aspect of most cities of the country. In many parts of small-town India, posters are pasted onto covered rickshaws that move about with a man making announcements over the loudspeaker. In the big cities, such older forms of film promotion are slowly being replaced with the arrival of new digital technologies and the powerful presence of neon-light advertisements in the streets. Unable to compete with the glittering lights of the new city, film posters seem

1. (*page 90*) *Guide* directed by Vijay Anand (1965).

2. Newspaper advertisement for *Raja Harishchandra* directed by Dadasaheb Phalke (1913).

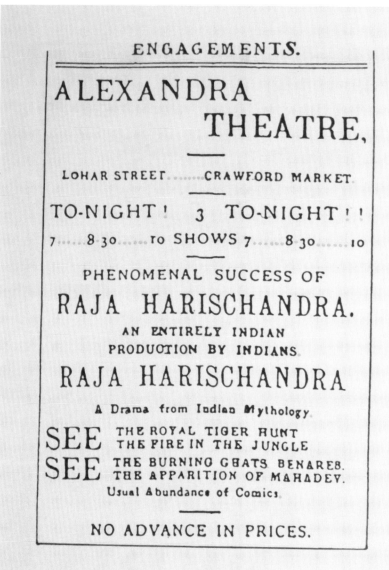

ENGAGEMENTS.

ALEXANDRA THEATRE,

LOHAR STREET.........CRAWFORD MARKET.

TO-NIGHT! 3 TO-NIGHT!!

7.....8 30.....TO SHOWS 7.....8 30.......10

PHENOMENAL SUCCESS OF

RAJA HARISCHANDRA.

AN ENTIRELY INDIAN PRODUCTION BY INDIANS

RAJA HARISCHANDRA

A Drama from Indian Mythology.

SEE THE ROYAL TIGER HUNT THE FIRE IN THE JUNGLE

SEE THE BURNING GHATS BENARES. THE APPARITION OF MAHADEV.

Usual Abundance of Comics.

NO ADVANCE IN PRICES.

Adv. of *Raja Harishchandra*, Silent, Phalke Films Dir. D G Phalke

Celebrated as India's first regular and indigenous feature film, it was released on May 3, 1913 at the coronation in Bombay. Phalke remade it in 1917.

3. *Kalyan Khajina* directed by Baburao Painter (1924).

to have moved away from the centre to the periphery. In Delhi for instance, posters are displayed primarily in the old city or in the dilapidated cinema halls of the eastern and western parts.[5] In small-town India, or what film distributors refer to as the "interiors", posters continue to be plastered on walls.

The film poster has always existed as a form that relies on distracted reception, as it is viewed by people during their travel within the city. It has constituted itself as a form of "street art" articulating a series of signs and symbols devised to arouse the curiosity of the passer-by. The urban landscape is a giant exhibition site within which the poster exists as one of the many elements that make up the semiotics of the city. As an iconic image, the poster is organized through a complex network of meanings that are produced, reproduced, contested, and negotiated from within the dynamic flux and flow of everyday life. Unlike calendar art, which is also a mass-printed form, the poster does not immediately have a buyer.[6] Because of its direct relationship to film publicity, the narrative composition of the poster is linked to practices of film production and distribution and like the form of popular cinema, the poster's semiotic value is created both internally and externally as it negotiates the industrial values of genre and stardom, audience expectation and desires.

Genre/stardom and imagining the audience

A combination of image and text, the poster works through a complex ordering of various elements that are based on an assumed hierarchy of information. For the designer, this hierarchy would be in the order of star/story/title and production credits. The textual material usually includes the names of producer, director, scriptwriter, music director, and lyricist. Stars and genres are two of the primary modes of meaning and pleasure offered by the film poster.[7] Genre implies a set of repetitive stylistic devices that help distinguish one set of films from another. Genre is also about the different ways in which producers, audiences, distributors, and critics create, organize, and interpret a system of visual signs.[8] Similarly, the film poster's production and circulation rely on a series of accepted codes that emerge out of the social and cultural life of both films and their posters.[9]

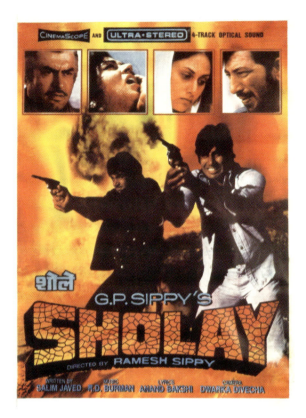

4 and 5. *Sholay* directed by Ramesh Sippy (1975).

Film posters in India negotiate themes of melodramatic conflict and action, romance and the family. Generic elements are compositionally arranged to reflect the multi-genre look of popular cinema. Simrat Brar, a well-known poster designer in the industry today, says that the film poster needs to cater to some form of categorization. Most films have four or five different posters, each negotiating a different thematic of the film. For *Lagaan* (Ashutosh Gowariker: 2001), Brar created three versions based on the different thematic elements of the film. The triangle love story was foregrounded in the first love story. Therefore Elizabeth (the Englishwoman) and Gracy Singh were profiled with Aamir Khan placed centrally within the frame. The second poster for *Lagaan* focused only on Aamir Khan and Gracy Singh's romance. The third version had a line-up of the village cricket team facing the camera. This was considered the most unusual. In retrospect Brar recognizes that the cricket team poster was not really spectacular but stood out amidst the clutter of other posters.[10] Similarly, stars have always played an important role in the compositional pattern of the poster. Modern publicity methods require a high degree of familiarity between the star and his/her potential audience. Several scholars have written

DHARMENDRA · SANJEEV KUMAR · AMITABH BACHCHAN
G. P. SIPPY'S
SHOLAY
IN 70 mm
STEREO PHONIC SOUND
DIRECTED BY
RAMESH SIPPY
WRITTEN BY
SALIM JAVED
MUSIC
R.D.BURMAN
LYRICS
ANAND BAKSHI
PHOTOGRAPHY
DWARKA DIVECHA

about the process that goes into the build-up of this familiarity which is worked out not just through the filmic image but also through a whole array of images generated by fan and gossip magazines, radio, television, newspapers, and the film poster.[11] Designed to make the star familiar and endearing for a wide public, the star becomes the central governing reference point for film publicity. Our access to the stars is also created through photographic still images like production stills, celebrity photos, press handbooks, interviews, reviews, and finally the film poster. All these images are generated during production and distribution and help to persuade and prolong the power of the moving image both before and after the release of a film.

In the 1970s when Amitabh Bachchan was the reigning superstar of the Bombay film industry, film posters either used Bachchan's singular image or foregrounded him as the dominant icon. *Deewar* (Yash Chopra: 1975) had several posters for its release. The story of two brothers, one a policeman, the other an outlaw, was established clearly in the posters through costume, posture, and demeanour. In one of the versions, Amitabh Bachchan was placed in the foreground standing in a defiant position looking directly at the spectator. Shashi Kapoor's face with his police inspector's cap was placed in the background. Bachchan's blue dock-worker shirt was recast as a red shirt in the poster. This was intended to make a connection with the red that is worn by "coolies" at railway stations and at the same time present the superstar in a colour that was more visually striking than the royal blue he actually wore in the film. *Coolie* (Manmohan Desai: 1983) has a poster that shows Bachchan in the centre of the frame, his red attire highlighted along with his badge number – 786 (the numerical total that stands for *Bismillah-e-Reheman-e-Rahim*). Here the poster relies on pre-existent knowledge available from his earlier films (the number 786 was used in *Deewar*, the film that catapulted Bachchan to stardom). Thus stars are presented through techniques that create a larger-than-life image enabling forms of identification within a wide film public.

Following design, around 150,000 posters are printed and then sent out to the various distribution territories directly by the printers.[12] India has five major distribution territories with Bombay (Mumbai) as the largest one. Given the scale of diversity and the vast interiors of the country, audiences are often segmented and fragmented according to what the distribution network sees as culturally and socially specific. Therefore the **A**, **B**, and **C** centres have come to represent three different streams of audience composition for the distributors. **A** centres constitute the big metros like Delhi, Mumbai, Kolkata, Bangalore, Chennai, and other big cities. **B** centres are the smaller towns, also known as the interiors, and **C** centres are the places where a special group of films, usually low-budget semi-porn films, circulate. The compositional life of a film poster in India depends on the way the distributor works through these territorial divisions. Sanjay Mehta, a leading film distributor based in Delhi, suggests that the "urban cosmopolitan" sensibility of the **A** centres gives the distributor some freedom with the poster. The use of a guitar in a poster may not be acceptable in the interiors. Therefore new sets of posters are usually designed locally to match the audience taste of the interiors. Mehta suggests that the guitar may be turned into a gun for the benefit of the **B**

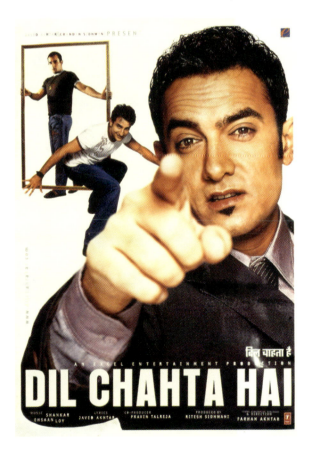

6. (*facing page*) *Lagaan* directed by Ashutosh Gowariker (2001).

7. *Dil Chahta Hai* directed by Farhan Akhtar (2001).

centre audiences.[13] Similarly the popularity of particular stars in certain regions can change the look of a poster. For distribution in the north Indian territory and the interiors, multi-starrer films with actors like Sunny Deol and Saif Ali Khan would be organized to highlight Deol's masculine presence. The principles of star power according to regional sensibilities and audience expectation work to influence the design of the poster just as they play a role in star decisions for particular films. Action films are usually considered successful in **B** centres and in some **A** centres. Therefore posters for action films highlight the melodramatic power of anger, the male body, guns, technology, cars, and stunts. In these posters the figure of the woman is fairly marginalized. In contrast the family films, a big staple of the **A** centres, highlight the carnivalesque aspects of the new Indian family, joyous celebration, coy gestures, colourful wedding attire, and the presence of many women. Romance plays a crucial role in the projection of the family films. Yash Chopra's family films which are usually successful with **A** centres, are considered appealing for their "soft, bubble gum, romantic look".[14] In these posters clothing, pastel colours, and a dreamlike fantasy disposition become important.

The network of knowledge that circulates between the production and reception of the poster constitutes a zone of co-authorship between the public/audience and the mediated product. The circulating mythology of what works and is acceptable enters the language and parlance of the film industry's marketing strategy and gets assimilated as "knowledge" of popular taste and the box office. While these perceptions obviously shape the actual production of films, their impact on poster culture is more dynamic. Once a film is released its fate is decided by the box office. Nothing can be done to change the film itself; steps can only be taken for future productions. The poster can however be continuously reinvented and worked upon to help the film get its maximum profit at the box office. Therefore the different versions of posters brought out during the running of a film offer us a fleeting glimpse into the way distributors, audiences, and stars negotiate the invisible terrain of desire, taste, pleasure, and expectation. The poster then does not simply exist as an object of use and exchange value. On the contrary

its life clearly indicates how it is marked by cultural, social, and cognitive processes that work to make it a particular kind of product.

Design technology, television, and urban space

Posters travel an elaborate journey as they move through techniques of production, design composition, layout, and the final printing process. In the past, photographs provided by the producer were creatively duplicated on canvas by painters. It took one week to design a hand-painted poster, which usually combined

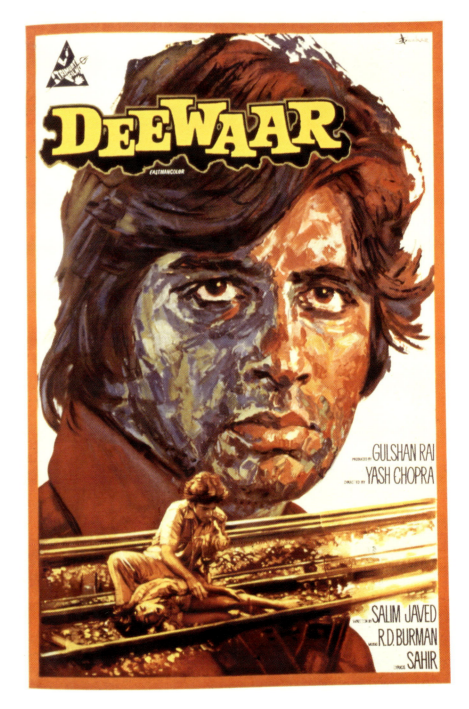

8 and 9. *Deewar* directed by Yash Chopra (1975).

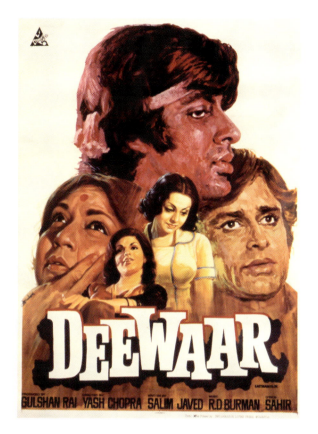

elements of action and stars, along with the credits. The artists were specialists in poster design. The average canvas image was 30 inches (75 centimetres) wide and 40 inches (1 metre) in length. In the absence of enlargement lenses, the size had to be the same as the final poster print. The canvas image was then photographed in natural sunlight using a traditional camera. The original design size was reduced after 1985 when new enlargement lenses arrived in India. This was followed by a period when the poster industry adopted what they popularly refer to as the "cut-and-paste" method. Film stills were cut out and compositionally arranged, and then the colour for the background and other embellishments were added with a paintbrush. Omkar Potdar recalls his entry into poster designing during the "cut-and-paste" period which started sometime in the 1960s. Since colour photography came to India only in the mid/late 1970s, black-and-white photographs were shot on location and then they were painted over with bold colours.[15] The "cut-and-paste" has therefore been a combination of the photographic and the painted.

The poster industry itself is an elaborate structure today that requires about 5 to 10 per cent of the overall budget of a film.[16] It is a crucial part of the print publicity package designed for every film.[17] There are seven or eight major poster design houses, all located in Mumbai.[18] Work is contracted to these design houses who then prepare the print publicity. The designers work through their ideas in consultation with the producer and the director. The designer is sometimes given the script and in the absence of one has to rely on the different ways in which the film is represented by its creators. The key issues that any designer would look for are songs, script, actors, and locations. The designer is also provided with many stills from the film. Studio and outdoor photo shoots are organized with the lead stars and then all the photographs are scanned. The process of selection takes days as the designer tries out different ways to layer and compose the posters with the available stills. The arrival of computer technology has made way for greater digital manipulation, forms of layering, colour correction, and multiple images. The ability to try out different compositions on the computer is seen to enable greater flexibility to represent the multiple dynamics of any film. Along with the breed of high-profile established designers in Mumbai, a parallel economy of local designers has emerged in other cities. These designers are comfortable with computer culture and regularly download star images from the internet to design local posters. The proliferation of computer shops of every kind has made accessibility to this technology easy. There are many former designers who are now sitting in computer shops, composing for election posters, low-budget films (particularly C circuit and local designs for the interiors), and government health campaigns.[19] Despite their creative skills, none of the local designers gets paid like their high-profile counterparts in Mumbai.

Trained as a designer at the National Institute of Design, Ahmedabad, Simrat Brar started her career in advertising. Today she is one of the leading designers of film posters. While the Bombay film poster has always had its own unique form of presentation, Brar recognizes that today the look of the poster, its design aesthetics, and paper quality are increasingly dependent on various trends within commercial advertising. Since many designers are now joining the film industry with a background in corporate advertising, the overlap

11. *Dil to Pagal Hai* directed by Yash Chopra (1997).

10. (*facing page*) *Dil Chahta Hai* directed by Farhan Akhtar (2001).

the eye's optical capacity to wander through diverse locations of the world. The proliferation of visual "surfaces" linked primarily to the spectacularization of consumerist display has transformed the nature of street interaction in some parts of the city, even as the coexistence with older forms of display continue to be present in other parts of the city. Whatever the exact nature of the transformation, the emergence of a distinctly different regime of visual culture cannot be denied since electronic surfaces and other forms of aestheticized display are creating a fascination for visual euphoria. Thus like the cinematic form itself, the poster has also acquired that distinctly "new" glossy look.

The coming of cable television in the 1990s created a new space for film publicity. Initially, song sequences were released for countdown shows. Soon organized short trailers were created to publicize the film. The trailers have to make their presence felt in the clutter of programming, advertising, and music. People from the world of advertising are now asked to make the trailers spectacular and dramatic. The trailers make sure that the audience is given an array of foreign locations, action, romance, music, and star presence. Having emerged as a prime site for film publicity, the relationship between television and the film industry has deepened as virtually all the channels are now showcasing "Bollywood". Rahul Nanda, the man responsible for introducing digital technology in 1992, literally wiped out the "cut-and-paste" method that was still prevalent at that time.[20] Nanda identifies television as the main reason for the "new look" of the poster. He saw the big painted hoardings as "kitsch", where "actors looked dirty, painted, and tacky". He introduced the first digitally created billboards in the city. For Nanda, film advertising "started looking classy and sophisticated" in the 1990s. Nanda faced initial resistance from traditional designers but computer technology finally became the dominant mode of poster designing. "Today print media can look like electronic media," says Nanda who sees the internet and global television as marking a new era where visual culture moves in a seamless loop between the print and the moving image.[21] Clearly the desire for gloss and sophistication is fuelled by a transformation of the visual scape that is visibly

of techniques is not surprising. The fluid movement between advertising and the film industry is also reflective of the new aesthetics of consumption emerging with globalization.

The visual force of globalization in India can easily be seen in the radical transformation of many urban spaces. The rise of multiplexes and refurbished movie theatres, the emergence of shopping malls, coffee shops, ATMs, and neon-light advertisements across the prime districts of many of the big cities have introduced a new regime of spectacle. Added to this is the transformation of both the home and the outside where cable television has in a dynamic way changed articulated in the arenas of architecture, advertising, film, and fashion.

As the texture of the built environment undergoes changes through novel uses of steel, glass, and light, we enter a zone of urban movement in certain parts of the city that is spectacularly aestheticized, magical, and seductive. One of the major additions to the built environment that we have seen in the last few years is the entry and presence of television. Television in its new incarnation has entered the dynamic rhythms of public life and space in seemingly unobtrusive ways. As both small and big shops, department stores, restaurants, coffee shops, bars, fast-food chains, airports, and other public spaces generate the visual culture of "ambient television", the perceptual sphere of the distracted gaze experiences the visual dynamics of the electronic media.[22] We encounter the television set in more places than just our home as it integrates itself within the rhythms of urban life. This pervasive and continuous interaction with the rapid movement of images, both at home and in public (in small towns and big cities) pushes the film poster to match the aesthetics and the shiny quality of the television screen and at the same time appear in a more organized and ordered pattern. Both Simrat Brar and Rahul Nanda have indicated how the look of the poster needs to overlap with the promos appearing on television. The visual impact of both forms need to be similar in order to create a seamless publicity loop. The spectacularization of urban display requires a different order of aesthetics since, as many have suggested, new technology has enacted ineradicable perceptual shifts in the spectacle. In this scenario, the hand-painted film poster, once ordinary, now a lost art, acquires the status of a unique "art" object.

Nostalgia and artistic aura in the digital age

Walter Benjamin, in his well-known thesis on the destruction of aura after the birth of the photograph, had envisioned a time when multiplication and mechanical reproduction would enable the possibility of art becoming a genuinely democratic form, accessible and available outside the rarified space of the art museum.[23] In a strange twist, the original hand-painted film poster which was seen plastered on walls in various parts of the country and available

for a price of five rupees in the streets till the early 1990s, has now acquired the status of an "art" form as collectors enter the field of preservation, display, and sale. This process can be seen as an instance of what Arjun Appadurai has described as commoditization by diversion where value is "accelerated or enhanced by placing objects and things in unlikely contexts". Appadurai suggests that this narrative of diversion rests on the commodity's removal from its customary circuits through a coming together of the "aesthetic impulse" and the "entrepreneurial link".[24]

Initially overlooked as an art form because of its direct relationship to commercial networks of publicity, today the gradual disappearance of the poster from the streets and public places where it had traditionally found a home, has made it a more respectable item to be studied, looked at, and placed within the rarified atmosphere of galleries and homes. Just as the photographic, digitally created image becomes the dominant icon in contemporary poster culture, the hand-painted, "authentic" "Bollywood" poster acquires auratic power as collectors and museums compete with their own collections. Collectors of artefacts and objects, posters and photographs, paintings and old books recognize the power of nostalgia within modernity. The collector engages in the process of diversion precisely to enhance the aesthetic power of his/her collection. The hand-painted film poster today is a collector's item, a commodity enclosed and rarified, a product of nostalgia, "entrepreneurial genius", popular memory, and modernity.

FIGURE ACKNOWLEDGEMENTS

Figures 2, 3, 8, and 9, courtesy National Film Archive of India, Pune; figures 1, 4–7, 10, 11 from the author's collection.

NOTES

[1] My research on the film poster has been made possible by the India Foundation for the Arts (IFA), Bangalore and the Fundacao Oriente, Lisbon/Goa. This is an abridged version of a longer essay first published in *Seminar*: May 2003.

[2] The biographical method adopted here is inspired by the work of Igor Kopytoff. See his "The Cultural Biography of Things: Commoditization as Process" in Arjun Appadurai (ed.),

The Social Life of Things: Commodities in Cultural Perspective, Cambridge: Cambridge University Press, 1986, pp. 64–91.

[3] Rachel Dwyer and Divia Patel, *The Visual Culture of Hindi Film*, New Brunswick, New Jersey: Rutgers University Press, 2002, p. 110.

[4] It is not my intention here to chart out a historical chronology of the different influences and artistic achievements of the poster. For a history of the development of the film poster see ibid.; Patel and Dwyer's chapter on film advertising presents us with the details of early film publicity and its transformation over time.

[5] The Bengal Act 21 of 1976, section 3(1) says "whoever defaces any property in public view by writing or marking with ink, chalk, paint or any other material,...shall be punishable with imprisonment...or with fines...or both". This was later extended to other states like Delhi. The implementation of this act has affected both Kolkata and Delhi. Mumbai continues to be a city where posters are regularly plastered on walls. Even in Delhi and Kolkata, there are many areas of the city, particularly the older parts, where posters can still be seen on the walls.

[6] For interesting accounts of the production and circulation of calendar art see Kajri Jain, "Of the Everyday and the National Pencil: Calendars in Postcolonial India", *Journal of Arts and Ideas*, Nos. 27–28, 1995. While Jain makes a distinction between the cinema and calendar art, she does see a similarity in the role and movement of the poster and calendars. I do believe the direct relationship to film publicity makes the poster somewhat different.

[7] For a fascinating and imaginative analysis of the posters of two films *Zimbo Finds a Son* (John Cavas: 1966) and *The Player* (Homi Wadia: 1960) see Rosie Thomas, "Zimbo and Son Meet The Girl with the Gun", in David Blamey and Robert D'Souza (eds.), *Living Pictures: Perspectives on the Film Poster in India*, London: Open Editions, 2005. Thomas's vivid dissection of the posters brings to the fore issues of sexuality, masculinity, stardom, and genre as central to the universe of the film posters' iconography. Further, she addresses the question of audience reception and perception to show the complex cultural circuits through which Hollywood signage is transformed within an Indian context.

[8] Toby Miller, *Technologies of Truth: Cultural Citizenship and the Popular Media*, Minneapolis and London: University of Minnesota Press, 1998, p. 18.

[9] The role of genre is clearly a universal phenomenon amply demonstrated through analysis of posters in other parts of the world like Hollywood, Mexico, and Turkey. See Rogelio Agrasanchez, "Poster Art from the Golden Era of Mexican Cinema", in *Archiro Filmico Agrasanchez, Universidad de Guadalajara Instituto Mexicano de Cinematografia*, 1997; and Steve Schapiro and David Chierichetti, *The Movie Poster Book*, New York: E.P. Dutton, 1979.

[10] Interview with Simrat Brar, designer for Glamour Publicity, Mumbai, November 2002.

[11] Christin Gledhill (ed.), *Stardom: Industry of Desire*, London: Routledge, 1991; Jacky Stacey, *Star Gazing: Hollywood Cinema & Female Spectatorship*, London: Routledge, 1994; Richard Dyer, *Heavenly Bodies*, New York: St Martins Press, 1986.

[12] Interview with Gul Sugandh, the owner of Glamour Publicity, Mumbai, November 2002 and with Saifi Shah of Silverpoint Press, the largest poster printing house in Mumbai, April 2003.

[13] Interview with Sanjay Mehta, Delhi, August 2002.

[14] Interview with Fayaz Badruddin, designer for Yashraj Films' Design Cell, Mumbai, November 2002.

[15] Interview with Omkar Potdar, poster designer, Mumbai, April 2003.

[16] Interview with Gul Sugandh, Glamour Publicity, Mumbai, November 2002.

[17] Posters are usually released in two batches. The first release is concurrent with the music/audio release, usually seen in music shops and electronic markets like Palika Bazaar in Delhi.

[18] Some of the well-known design houses are: Glamour, H.R. Enterprises, Abel & Will, Studio Links, Epigram, and Endeavour.

[19] Interview with Ajay Kapoor, printer, Delhi, February 2003.

[20] The "cut-and-paste" method is still prevalent in the local designs of some of the smaller budget films, particularly in the C circuit.

[21] Interview with Rahul Nanda, H.R. Enterprises, Mumbai, November 2002.

[22] The term is taken from Anna McCarthy's work on the role of television in public life. See her *Ambient Television: Visual Culture & Public Space*, Durham & London: Duke University Press, 2001.

[23] "The Work of Art in the Era of Mechanical Reproduction", in *Illuminations*, New York: Schocken Books, 1969, pp. 217–51.

[24] Appadurai (ed.), *The Social Life of Things*, p. 28.

THE FAMILY ARCHIVE photo

Savia Viegas

Historians of 19th-century photography have become increasingly concerned with examining and clarifying photography's role in the context of colonialism and imperialism.[1] New processes of enquiry have directed research away from master narratives – those corresponding to a single reading of events – and have sought multiple interpretations, ones that allow for alternative, even contradictory, viewpoints that more accurately reflect history's inherent complexity. In the case of British colonial history, there is widespread scholarly acknowledgement of the symbiotic relationship between economic demands and political priorities in determining policies and shaping attitudes. There is a danger that the specificities of the larger historical landscape and the spectacular saga of photography in British India may be used to define the same in Goa, as has been a major pitfall with the imagination of national history. Even Edward Said has shown, in his monolithic treatise, that his work on Orientalism[2] does not cover the contribution of Germany, Italy, Russia, Spain, and Portugal. Though the Goan experience under the Portuguese remains understated, it is nonetheless both important and unique and yields a different reading.

The physical presence of the Portuguese in the Estado de India was very limited, necessitating dependence on native Goan educated elites for filling administrative, ecclesiastical, and military positions. The Iberian rulers created a large infrastructure of primary-level educational institutions paving the way for a highly educated intelligentsia among the elite. The demand for higher education necessitated travel to educational centres at Belgaum, Dharwar, Bangalore, Poona, and Bombay which were then ruled by the British. The availability of jobs was not commensurate with the number of educated people and this was the single most important factor responsible for a mass exodus of educated Goans to parts of India then ruled by the British, and later to the East African colonies of Africa Inglesa. Many of these were from the landed elite – Chardo and Brahman caste but there were also others in proportionately small numbers. The proselytizing zeal of the rulers not only accounted for a large Catholic population but also created a population of keen travellers eager to strike it rich overseas and

not hindered by the cultural baggage of their Hindu Indian counterparts.

By the late 18th century Portugal was a sagging military power, impoverished, corrupt, and economically unstable. And by the time photography was introduced in the public domain in Europe (namely in France and Britain in 1839), the Portuguese – the earliest colonialists in the Indian context – were relegated to the peripheries of the subcontinent. Unlike British-ruled India where photography was introduced in 1840 and became a tool for imperial surveillance and documentation, the medium made its presence felt two decades later in Goa. Several painters travelling through the British Empire to capture the exotic colours and pristine landscapes of the tropics had also chanced upon Goa and the "Goanese", but with the invention of the photographic technique and its several improvisations a new dynamic of capturing the image set in. Between 1855 and about 1880, collodion/albumen technology made it possible for enterprising photographers, both amateur and professional, to follow their countrymen to Africa, the Americas, and other parts of Asia in order to record, besides scenery, aspects of daily life and ethnic customs.[3]

With the coming of the camera, a certain democratization of the image became possible as a

2. Segundo Dia (second day) of the marriage of Dr Maurilio Furtado Varca, 1960. This is the day after the nuptial night when the couple formally visits the girl's home to partake in traditional festivities. Photographer unknown.

1. (*previous pages*) Wall of family home of Dr Samiro Vaz with hunting photographs, Orlim. Photograph: Savia Viegas.

wide range of studios offered services that catered to most pockets.[4] Unlike the experience of North America where European emigres domesticating the Wild West and forming a new industrial working class clamoured, even paying half their weekly wage, to get a daguerreotype image of themselves to be sent to kin in Europe, in the Asiatic colonies of Britain and Portugal it was the new elites who made self and family portraits. Photography received wide patronage among the landed and the educated upwardly mobile who utilized the moods of painting when having themselves captured in black and white. In Goa the experience was even more unique as it had never known a decadent royalty, eclipsed as it was by a new ascending force of colonialism (exceptions were the Raja of Sonda and chiefdoms like that of the Desprabhus of Pernem or the Ranes of Sanquelim). Hence there are no photographs of royal splendour as is the case with other Indian photographs replete with native opulence.

But what Goa did have were feudal landed elites striking it rich from the earnings of rice and coconuts and a convenient system of land tenancy known as the Mundkar system. This system allowed them to cultivate a lifestyle of ease and self-sufficiency. The proselytization process was activated in 1559 backed by a decree from the Portuguese Crown that every male should convert, and render compulsory naval service, or surrender his lands to the Empire. The rich landed families, cornered by this harsh diktat adopted a counter-solution. Some members of the family emigrated along with their Hindu family deities to the borders of contiguous Hindu territories, while one brother and his family stayed on the ancestral property and converted to Christianity to retain control and possession of family lands.

In time other Goan elites adopted similar pragmatics: one son would be an agriculturist, another a priest, and a third would seek his fortune overseas in the colonies of the British Empire or in erstwhile Africa Portuguesa. Yet another might be a lawyer or a doctor. The solidarity of the extended family was an emotion very integral to Goa and each member contributed to manoeuvring the family towards social visibility and economic power. The presence of a lawyer in the family allowed for a close monitoring of sale of lands which the family could acquire.[5] Placement in service abroad brought the family capital; a career in medicine earned social respectability; and of course a son in the priesthood also gave enormous power and respectability. The agriculturist could then multiply family income. When you ask rich Bhatkars, rural land owners, why they did not emigrate as a good 20 per cent of the educated population did, the answer is representative of the situation: "I had to protect the family properties otherwise all would be lost."

But the colonized modernized easily took to refashioning themselves on the role model of European society (figure 2), adopting its airs and even perhaps imagining a mythic European ancestor. Historically there is no evidence in Goa of miscegenation on the scale that occurred in Brazil, Mexico, and other parts of Central and South America. As stated earlier the representation of the Portuguese on the mainland was small and hardly afforded such opportunities, which were further limited by local resistance.

Goan society has been subject to misrepresentation and stereotyping earlier during colonialism and later by the media and tourism industry,[6] so Goan social history has to be carefully sifted to circumvent

3. Dr Max Loyola Furtado with family album, Chinchinim. Photograph: Savia Viegas.

4. The house of Jorge Pereira-Gomes in Orlim, Salcete, now a home for nuns. Photograph: Savia Viegas.

5. Detail of the base of the column of the Pereira-Gomes *balcao*. Photograph: Savia Viegas.

typecasting. I chose to make the field my archive, first as a methodological strategy and second to be able to recapture how within the confines of the studio, or within the limits of the box, the elites had reframed images of themselves. In the frame of a photograph what the subject wants to retain as memory is made permanent by the authority of the photographer and for the viewer it becomes an archive through which a labyrinthine memory can be retrieved. Archives are cultural artefacts which encompass the past and the present. Undoubtedly, their interpretation may stand altered by the passage of time. To reconstruct social history it is important to include landscapes of towns and cities, domestic as well as public architecture (figures 4 and 5), to cull the sense of representation of order and authority in society and to be able to verify the legitimate authority of photographs as visual documents.

After its introduction in the 19th century, photography became very popular among the elite classes in Goa. Many of the photographs in family archives are still in use today, treasured, displayed, and often revered as relics of a past (figure 3). Some of them that depict ancestral relatives who held

important positions with the government or mothers who yielded illustrious sons enjoy optimum display at significant sites like the *sala* – the formal entertaining room which showcases the family's prize furniture and antiques (figure 6). Often the frames are eroded and the photographs disintegrating and in need of restoration, but nonetheless these artefacts valorize the crumbling

6. Photographic display of a maternal ancestor in the *sala* of the Dr Assis Fernandes home. Photograph: Savia Viegas.

to a general, and could maintain 120 soldiers. Some of the chairs depicted in the photograph are still used by the family. All the three sisters were married at the time, two having married into the Carvalho family of Betalbatim. Dr Martin Carvalho had died by the time the photograph was taken, and the two brothers-in-law hold up his photograph behind his hapless widow. The women's garments resemble Franciscan robes and the men sport handlebar moustaches in the fashion of the day. The Fernandes family was reputed to be very devout and god-fearing. Prayer service would be held early every morning and the family members would rise at an unearthly hour to pray together (figure 9). Octogenarian Posciano Rebello recalls his childhood reluctance to spend nights at the Fernandes home primarily because of this habit. Most of the families vied with each other to build family chapels which often matched the grandeur of altars and reredos in the church, with gold-leaf work and images of ivory. While such grandeur spoke of the status of the family, it also made visible its link to the Church which contributed to its power. In the construction of the social identity of the Roman Catholic population, the link with the Church was a crucial benchmark.

Vidya Dehejia argues that there is no such thing as an innocent historical eye. Photographs of India by early British photographers certainly reveal much about the world of India; but they reveal to an equal degree British attitudes towards the world.[7] Interestingly Goan photographs reveal, to borrow a phrase from Dehejia, Goan attitudes to themselves and to the world.

How did a hierarchized Goan society realign/reframe its internal social stratification under colonialism? What kind of imagery did it use to retain the rhetoric of its power under changed socioeconomic and political and even religious circumstances? During the second half of the 19th century, a fundamental tension developed between uses of photography that fulfil a bourgeois conception of self and the uses that seek to establish and delimit the terrain of the other.[8] The issues and challenges facing Victorian England were transported to the colonies where they were absorbed by the native populations as the ideology of the progressive era. At the same time photography as a medium of

walls and lend authority to a family eclipsed of its power, subordinating its present to its past.

Educated Goans played a crucial role in the building of Goan identity – masculine as well as traditional feminine. Photography gives visibility to the nuclear family as a conjugal and the extended family as a social unit, both roles being vital to the creation of Goan identity (figure 7). The link with the Church and the family house were important markers of the family wealth and hierarchy and conscious efforts were expended towards developing and maintaining both. Photographs captured vignettes of the family in transition. The photograph from the Fernandes family collection in Colva taken around 1890 shows three daughters posing in the maternal family *sala* in Colva (figure 8). The Fernandes family were bestowed the title of *Mestre de Campo*, the military post equivalent

7. Portrait of the Antao family from Betalbatim taken against the background of their ancestral home. Circa 1910. Photographer unknown.

8. The Fernandes sisters posing with their husbands in their maternal home in Colva, with a portrait of Dr Martin Carvalho, 1890. Photographer unknown.

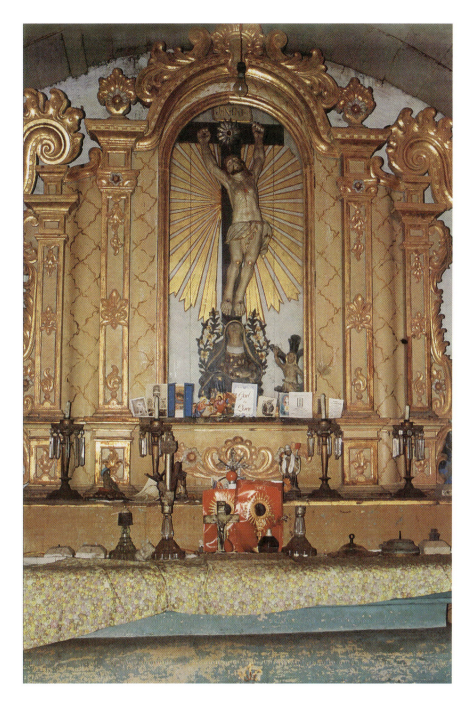

themselves in commissioned studio portraits just as whites did.[9]

This was the other way that the photographic medium allowed the colonized subject to recreate the world of power that the rulers played out; to transform the colonized land and use the same setting to create a hierarchical scaffolding for himself from where he addressed not those above him but those below him. Let me explain this further with the help of photographs. Many of the subjects on view in the Goan photographs with their quaint Victorian settings in the tropics may have never travelled abroad for education or even for pleasure. The photographic representation is clearly addressed to indigenous social hierarchies. A photograph from the Viegas family taken in 1920 shows the three siblings, i.e. two married sisters and the brother with child on his lap, and wife, sitting for a family portrait in the front yard of the family home, which till then had not been fully constructed (figure 10). The mother of the three siblings, though alive at the time, did not pose in the photograph. The right-hand side of the photograph shows a ladder and agricultural implements which are partially covered by the backdrop. The carpet on which the slave girl sits is evidently borrowed or has been provided by the travelling photographer. By the sham Victorian setting, clothes, hairstyles, and gaze, the family creates a representation through which it borrows some of the power and currency embedded in the setting while remaining rooted in its own social milieu.

Roland Barthes states that we look straight through the photograph, ignoring its status as signifier and seeing only the signified – the image itself.[10] The photograph like the footprint, is treated as an actual "trace" – an artefact of the scene that it reveals. Likewise, this photograph carries a subtext and is a Barthesian signifier. Elitism requires an otherness to become visible, in this case the slave in the photograph whose presence makes the status of the family visible. Slavery was banned in 1761 in mainland Portugal but it continued unopposed in the colonies till the 1930s and even the 1940s.

The Viegas family photograph creates this setting

9. Family altar of Dioguinho Fernandes Home, Colva. Photograph: Savia Viegas.

self-representation had given great visibility to the middle classes.

Photography in Goa functioned in two different worlds: the world of the dominant colonizer and that of the natives in the Estado de India with their multifarious circuits of hierarchy and power relations; from the newly proselytized converts to the white identity of the European colonizer whose paradigms and concerns the upwardly mobile highly educated Goan made his own. As Coco Fusco points out, in the early days of photography, non-white people reinvented

10. The Viegas family
from Carmona taken
at residence, 1920.
Photographer unknown.

addressed to the feudal tenured structure that the flowery backdrop tries to hide. This is not a wealthy family. The man in the photograph is the first educated member of the family and, taking on a primary school teaching position, he uses all his surplus income to acquire land and expand his house. In his lifetime, the house acquires a grand *sala*, *entrada*, and the wooden *galleria* and *balcao*. With these extensions and embellishments to his house he acquires the grandeur of the elite. The household includes his three daughters, wife, and a married sister who returns on being widowed to do agricultural labour along with the wage workers and tenants on their very modest landholdings, to be able to have rice and coconuts for domestic consumption. He himself does physical labour on his retirement but to distinguish the fact that he is a teacher he always wears old gabardine suits even when assisting at the plough or stacking the haystack for his cows.[11]

Hunting backdrops form a very popular theme of photographs taken in the 1930s and 40s (figure 1). One photograph shows the subject wearing boots, hunting trousers, and shirt, against a wooded backdrop, with a pistol pointed directly at the viewer (Introduction figure 9). It has been taken at Lord's Studio, Margao. Another shows Dr Samiro Vaz with a leopard carcass he shot in the wooded hills of Duessua, while a third

I presume has been shot on site. Woods and forests were a typical 18th-century trope to express fear and lurking danger, and such metaphorical imagery shows a gentrified Goan taste for sports leisure which is very European. Folksongs and *mando*s of the same time image the forest as a potential hideout for armed white soldiers on the prowl. The narrative is garnished with some amount of sexual innuendo:

Farar far zatai ranatum
Edi ratiche pakle bhovtai haddache
Main mhojea philoz khelai ghoddache.[12]

The woods resound with gunshots
In the deep of night the bearded white
   soldiers roam
My mother has prepared jaggery sweetmeats.

These photographs taken around the 1940s were modelled on a very feudal trope of European country life that ironically was fast eroding in the continent itself as the West industrialized and urbanized rapidly. Besides, the two world wars had rapidly pauperized and diminished the opulent lifestyle of European country life. In Goa an idyllic image, frozen against a pastoral backdrop, was museumized and lived beyond itself.

NOTES

[1] The documentary photograph as a work of art: see "American Photographs 1860 1876" in Vidya Dehejia (ed.), *India through the lens: photography 1840–1911*, Washington DC: Smithsonian Institution and Ahmedabad: Mapin Publishing, 2000, p. 127.

[2] Edward Said, *Orientalism*, Harmondsworth: Penguin, 2003, p. 17.

[3] Naomi Rosenblum, *A World History of Photography*, New York: Abbeville Press Publishers, 1997, p. 168.

[4] Malavika Karlekar, *Revisioning the Past: Early Photography in Bengal 1875–1915*, New Delhi: Oxford University Press, 2005, p. 2.

[5] The annual land taxes were high for the times and draconian measures were used against defaulters. The amount doubled with the fines and inability to pay for two simultaneous years resulted in seizure of lands. These lands were auctioned off and the trading was as brisk as that of the stock exchange today. Thus it was helpful to know law and have a family member in the administrative services.

[6] Goans were misrepresented as being cooks, ayahs, and butlers in many colonial references especially by the British. The Portuguese referred to them as *canarins* – an apellation with strong undertones of being weak and effeminate. On account of the colonial past and the social attitudes that it had bequeathed, the post-Independence stereotypes of Goans in the media were represented by dress, dating etiquettes, and socialization patterns, the Goan male often being depicted as a well meaning do-gooder, a victim of circumstance, and of an alcoholic disposition – typified by the song from *Majboor*, *"Michael daru pike danga karta hai!"* [Michael gets drunk and makes a ruckus!]

[7] Dehejia, *India through the lens*, p. 21.

[8] Allan Sekula in Coco Fusco and Brian Wallis (eds.), *Only Skin Deep – changing visions of the American self*, New York: International Center for Photography and Harry N. Abrams Inc, 2003, p. 80.

[9] Ibid., p. 40.

[10] Roland Barthes, *Camera lucida*, London: Flamingo Fontana Paperbacks, 1984.

[11] Fieldwork in Carmona in 2006. Episodes were narrated by an ex-pupil of his at the escola primaria, who is presently in his 80s.

[12] Verse from a popular Goan *dulpod*.

THE ENCLAVED GAZE explor
"world

Christiane Brosius

The social, economic and geographic divide in India is not a new phenomenon. But the transformation in "globalised" India has given the divide a new edge. There is now what is best called *Enclave India* that at work, home, schooling, and recreation is cut off from the larger India – figuratively and sometimes even literally. The citizens of Enclave India at the upper echelons work in office environments that rival the best in the world, often live in gated communities, the children go to "international" schools and they entertain themselves by visiting malls, multiplexes, and amusement parks or taking a holiday abroad.[1]

The focus of this paper is how, what Reddy has termed as both "globalised" and "Enclave India" is imagined, visualized, and sanctioned in and through lifestyle aesthetics. In this process, lifestyle concepts and practices are made "real", desirable, and available for particular experiences of members of the aspiring and affluent urban middle classes in India as well as returning and investment-oriented non-resident Indians (NRIs). The visual material drawn upon here surfaces in advertisements promoting life in gated townships, it appears in lifestyle and real-estate magazines, newspapers, builders' brochures, and on hoardings along major roads. To me, those visions of "globalized India" consist of an interesting assemblage of particular cosmopolitan and folkloristic distinctions that imbue what I term the "enclaved gaze".[2] The deregulation of the market economy in the early 1990s increased the circulation and availability of such images and lifestyles linked to the idea of the "good life" as an ongoing choreography of the upwardly mobile middle classes, invoking status-oriented ideals of individual mobility, affluence, and internationality. The new script that speaks through the lifestyle images under survey here reassures its beholder that India has finally freed herself from the stern dogma of five-year plans, from the stigma of being an underdeveloped nation, and that the country is now smoothly integrating into "world class" networks of living, trade, and investment. In the notion of a "global Indian lifestyle" apparent paradoxes such as tradition and modernity, history and present, fuse harmoniously. Thus, we find the familiar beside the new, the "Indian" next to the "foreign", and exotic or even eroticized associations. The images of this kind of popular culture surface and move like nomads through various public domains, crossing various borders in time and space: thus, Egyptian kings and Hindu deities, Indian and African beauties, Greek antiquity and English landscape gardens promote – and make real – a sense of both national and cosmopolitan identity, enabling a "vision of the Indian nation based on an idealized depiction of the urban middle classes and new patterns of commodity consumption",[3] at the same time both liberalized and gated.

Making a place for the "modern maharajas"

The first time I came to Gurgaon, one of the boom-towns of India's privatized economy, I was perplexed, besides all the visual stimulations and spatial experiences offered by shopping malls, modern office blocks, condominiums, and construction sites, by a

1. (*previous pages*) "Unveiling the Art of Timeless Living" Ansals' Florence Marvel, Gurgaon, 2005.

2. Negolice's Victoria Gardens, Delhi. Advertisement in *Jetwings*, October 2006, p. 175.

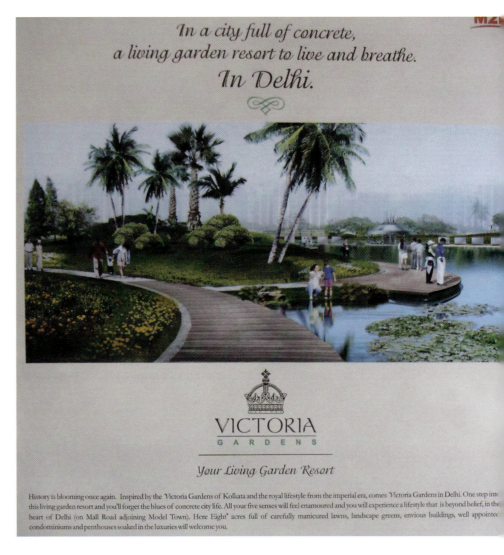

In a city full of concrete, a living garden resort to live and breathe. *In Delhi.*

VICTORIA
G A R D E N S

Your Living Garden Resort

History is blooming once again. Inspired by the Victoria Gardens of Kolkata and the royal lifestyle from the imperial era, comes Victoria Gardens in Delhi. One step into this living garden resort and you'll forget the blues of concrete city life. All your five senses will feel enamoured and you will experience a lifestyle that is beyond belief, in the heart of Delhi (on Mall Road adjoining Model Town). Here Eight' acres full of carefully manicured lawns, landscape greens, envious buildings, well appointed condominiums and penthouses soaked in the luxuries will welcome you.

DISCOVER THE IDEAL LAND!

3. Gulmohur Greens, SVP Group. This luxury condominium built by SVP Builders Ltd is located close to the East Delhi-UP border. From a lifestyle magazine, January 2007.

Yet, by scrolling through newspapers or real-estate journals and gazing at the booming satellite cities of megacities like Kolkata, Delhi, or Bangalore, and smaller cities like Lucknow, Jaipur, or Amritsar, the eye of the beholder encounters a plethora of similar depictions that are staged for the pleasure of consumption. The viewer is offered visions and views of a "five-star life" with the promise of 24-hour security, water, and electricity, a club house, swimming pool, and fitness centre, maybe even a hospital and a school. The items and places on display, catalysing imaginations and desires, are just part of a whole range of new pleasures and spaces that have cumulatively emerged since the 1990s and intensified in this millennium. Some of the visually most eye-catching examples available in 2-D are luxury villas in Gurgaon such as Ansals' Florence Marvel, SVP Group's Gulmohar Greens, or Negolice's Victoria Gardens (figures 1–3). The advertisements present festively lit individual villas with huge windows, balconies, and terracotta tiles, possibly topped by a roof-garden. They show blocks of high-rise buildings assembled around a park with green lawns, flowerbeds, lakes or swimming pools, and shady trees. As points of identification, people feature too: we may see a man dressed in a Western suit as he meditates on spacious lawns, or a young couple gazing out of an apartment building, giving a bird's-eye perspective onto an area covered by dozens of other high-rise buildings; or couples and nuclear families enjoying a stroll in a lush and exotic park named after a site in the former colonial capital, Kolkata.

These visual quotations often come to life only after they merge in the viewer's mind and when exhibited along with a plethora of slogans. Reads the ad for Ansals' Florence Marvel at the construction site in Gurgaon's Sushant Lok (figure 1): "Unveiling the Art of Timeless Living. Ansals' Florence Marvel. Luxurious Villas with personal swimming pool, golf putting greens & open air bar on the terrace." A newspaper version carries the additional line, "*Inviting those who belong to class. See it, to believe it!*" Underlining these associations is the projection of a competent and self-conscious consumer with "classic", "eternal" good taste and global way of life, a true cosmopolitan. The references to golf, a sport that invites relaxation and

hoarding of a township called Sahara Grace. Then, in early 2006, the hoarding was placed beside one of the boomtown's malls and entitled *For the Modern Maharajas*. Despite all the other hoardings and the buzzing visual and spatial dynamics of the trendy M.G. Road (connecting Delhi with Gurgaon), this particular board stood out for various reasons. Partly I was struck by the inherent contradiction of the hoarding: I associated maharajas with a nostalgic grandeur of large palaces set in pre-colonial and colonial history rather than state-of-the-art and high-rise apartment blocks made of concrete, one of many among commercial condominiums and other private guarded communities. Likewise, my attention was caught by the confidence of an elitist rhetoric addressing a growing audience of people who bought into the seemingly contradictory vision of modernity paired with the nostalgic one of royalist and national identity.

business conversations, and to people who would regularly host garden or roof terrace parties equipped with the open-air bar on the terrace for regular parties (also indicating the growing acceptance of alcohol as signifier of Westernized sophistication), are suggestive of the luxurious "high life". In conclusion, the addressee of the advertisement is assumed to have the confidence, or at least the desire, to *belong to class*. "Belonging to class" means "to be special" or "to have made it", to be part of a trendsetting transnational elite immersed in impression management. As a seemingly distinct style it also indicates that there are certain visible signs and ways of placing them strategically, creating the notion of a clear-cut border between those who belong and those who don't, the haves and the have-nots. In his book on images and lifestyle, Stuart Ewen argues that the notion of "being special", in particular the "feeling" of being exclusive, is crucial to the development of lifestyle aspirations acquired through advertisement images by the middle classes. This requires a distinguishable set of "images, attitudes, acquisitions, and style". And even if "the 'life-style' ... is not realizable in life, it is nevertheless the most constantly available lexicon from which many of us draw the visual grammar of our lives".[4] In this context, images of status and style, e.g. strategies of distinction, become the social currency and the symbolic and cultural capital in an increasingly mobile and fluid commercialized and globalized world whose members want all but move downwards.[5]

Besides the rapid and drastic changes in the media landscape, deregulation of the market, and introduction of capitalist institutions such as real-estate developers, shopping malls, or leisure theme parks have drastically changed the urban landscape and notions of lifestyle and introduced new social categories and groups, for instance the "single" or the "metrosexual". Such specifications aside, it seems noteworthy that the new middle class imagined in this and the following advertisements, and its "visual lexicon" of identification converges with a "new transnational cosmopolitan class of Indians", a phrase coined by Ronald Inden.[6] Their Arcadian visions of lifestyle, as Inden argued in his analysis of the Hindi blockbuster *Hum Aapke Hain Kaun...!* (1994), are set in worlds where "the masses have virtually disappeared. Only the elite are present." Whether filmi heroes and heroines or modern maharajas, they all float playfully in a "suburban utopia".[7] Thus, the visual popular language of Bollywood and Gurgaon share the same imaginary, developing a similar "enclaved gaze" that excludes the majority of Indians who do not (or must not) have any access to "world class". The visibility of the Self produces the invisibility of the Other, or, as we shall see below, avails of the latter for exotic consumption.

In "real-time", the consumers of the lifestyle visualities and visibilities are white-collar employees and professionals from the information technology or retail sector, queuing up for jobs in, or already working for, one of the mushrooming IT offices, call centres, and MNCs. Though they may have never lived abroad, their enclaved gaze of "world class" standards and goods of living has been shaped and sharpened by satellite television, lifestyle magazines, shopping malls. They care for both, the "Indian touch" and "internationality" or "world class", the urban and the religious or folkloristic. Imported, "foreign" commodities, increasingly available after the liberalization of the market economy, are crucial to the discourses and self-esteem of the new middle classes.

A key notion in this context is "global". Real-estate developers such as Ansals or Assotech circulate their message with images such as in their advertisement "Eleganté – Global living for global Indians" (figure 4). We learn that "A global concept deserves a global audience". And we see how a young couple, the "modern maharajas", look out of the grand window of their flat in a high-rise apartment building. Their gaze falls onto a cityscape that could be located anywhere from Singapore, to Dubai or Shanghai – or a completely imaginary "non-place",[8] a place for imagination in transit and montaged. More important than the actuality of the *topos* is that in its appearance, it seems somehow delocalized, "a place that's truly international!" Then we learn (and try to imagine), that a German kitchen with *white goods* as well as a *sky lounge for unique cosmic experience* come as part and parcel with the *lifestyle facilities,* and that launches of these apartment buildings have simultaneously been

4. "Global Living for Global Indians". Assotech Eleganté. Advertisement printed in a lifestyle journal, 2005.

held in hubs along what could be called the "diasporic lifestyle axis", that is, in Dubai, the USA, and Canada. By now we can sense that the audience is made up of a new "species" of Indians. Their members represent the ongoing miles-and-more traveller or "career nomad", who touches ground according to the availability of lucrative jobs and work permits, in India or abroad, with increasingly fluctuating residential addresses and high expectations in adequate lifestyle environments. Many of them might have turned into fairly wealthy

employees at high speed – and it is in particular these "newcomers" who seek guidance in the vast infrastructure of lifestyle and "taste" experts.

To have all the trendy and necessary facilities to live a good and beautiful life, in a centrally located and well-connected place, among others who think and live alike and yet still independent, seems ideal. This vision is also reflected in the next advertisement that appeals to the affluent and mobile consumer's desire to live

ASSOTECH
Building future.

Global living for global Indians

A global concept deserves a global audience.

Assotech launches Eleganté simultaneously in the USA, Canada, Dubai and India.

Presenting Eleganté - Global living for global Indians, from Assotech. Located within the Windsor Park and replete with almost all modern amenities, these ultra luxurious homes inspired by international way of living are an ode to luxury. Conceived and designed to bring global living standards to India, it's a place that's truly international!

"the way the world lives", as in the case of Victoria Gardens in New Delhi. In the montage, couples with and without children are portrayed walking through an exotic Garden City, with palm trees, lakes, flowers; the skyscraper residential blocks blurred, hardly visible, at the horizon (figure 2). The images of lifestyle in urban India paint a utopian picture in which members of the established and new affluent upper middle classes can safely dwell, without the alleged hassles of everyday life in the "chaotic and unsafe" city outside. The notion of living abroad becomes a portable item as exemplified in the following excerpt from an advertisement by Opera Garden Luxury Apartments & Penthouses: "get ready to live abroad in India!" (*TOI Property Supplement*, January 13, 2007). Such a heterotopic site, or "privatopia",[9] secluded from the everyday garb of the public, is also promised to the potential buyers of a gated township called Vatika City, in Gurgaon:

> For some a Home is more than just an address. It's a statement. .... Live the way the world's jet-set prefers. ... [apartments] nestled amidst contemporary townscape architecture and located within the lush settings of Vatika City. Artistically designed for the discerning few, the limited edition apartments speak of opulence and extravagance. ... Fully air-conditioned. Hermetically sealed, sound proof environs [sic!]. ... State-of-the-art security.[10]

This is a strange combination of desires of the "world's jet-set" and the "discerning few", showing how closely tied totalitarian security and individual freedom, spatial exclusion and inclusion, the longing for prestige and respectability, and social anxieties can be. The outside world is "switched off". Instead, life only happens behind well-guarded walls and under video-surveillance, as in another example of a prime real-estate developer and builder (figure 3). According to anthropologist Caldeira, writing on South American walled communities of middle and upper classes, these people display a longing for independence and freedom "both from the city and its mixture of classes". She further writes that "a new aesthetic of security shapes all types of constructions and imposes its new logic of surveillance and distance as a means for displaying status, and

it is changing the character of public life and public interactions".[11] Thus, the enclaved gaze of "hermetically sealed, sound proof environs", in toto underlining the images discussed so far, is also imbued with the anxiety, or fear, or being disturbed, threatened, if not swallowed up, by a disorderly, uncontrollable public. Through the lens of the enclaved gaze, the integration into the global community seems of more relevance and is perceived as more familiar and "natural" than the local worlds of the bazaar or the *gali* (alleyway). The world "out there" is a world that must be either successfully disciplined and tamed by "strategic embellishment" or ignored and neglected.[12]

Staging themed histories and traditions

Another dominant theme in the visual culture of "world class" living, besides the global Indian, is the storehouse of (transcultural) history and tradition, both neatly tied to particular values that those who execute the enclave gaze (should) possess. The enclave world must offer all one wants in terms of "daily needs" such as beauty parlour, supermarket, fitness centre, even a hospital; it is a "world en miniature", a "world exhibition" glorifying the commodity fetish.[13] But beyond that, it must trigger off desires, attract attention, and entertain the beholder by means of a theme or a mega-narrative. And instead of reminding him/her of India's stigma as a developing state, many of the enclave narratives are interlinked with a nostalgic projection of a national Golden Age and the longing to revitalize this through festive pomp and religious traditions.

As mentioned above, new places and experts offer impression and lifestyle-management services, giving all kinds of reasons why, and advice on how, life should be conducted in certain ways. The display of wealth and self-esteem requires care and competence. "History" gives depth and feeling to nationality and cosmopolitanism. And the accumulation of historical items affirms one's prestige and taste. There is, for instance, a fascination with historical architecture, ancient sites, and town planning. Reads the text for the Victoria Gardens advertisement: "History is blooming once again. Inspired by the Victoria Gardens of Kolkata and the royal lifestyle from the imperial era, comes

5. Eros Rosewood City (Eros Grand Mansions II), Gurgaon.

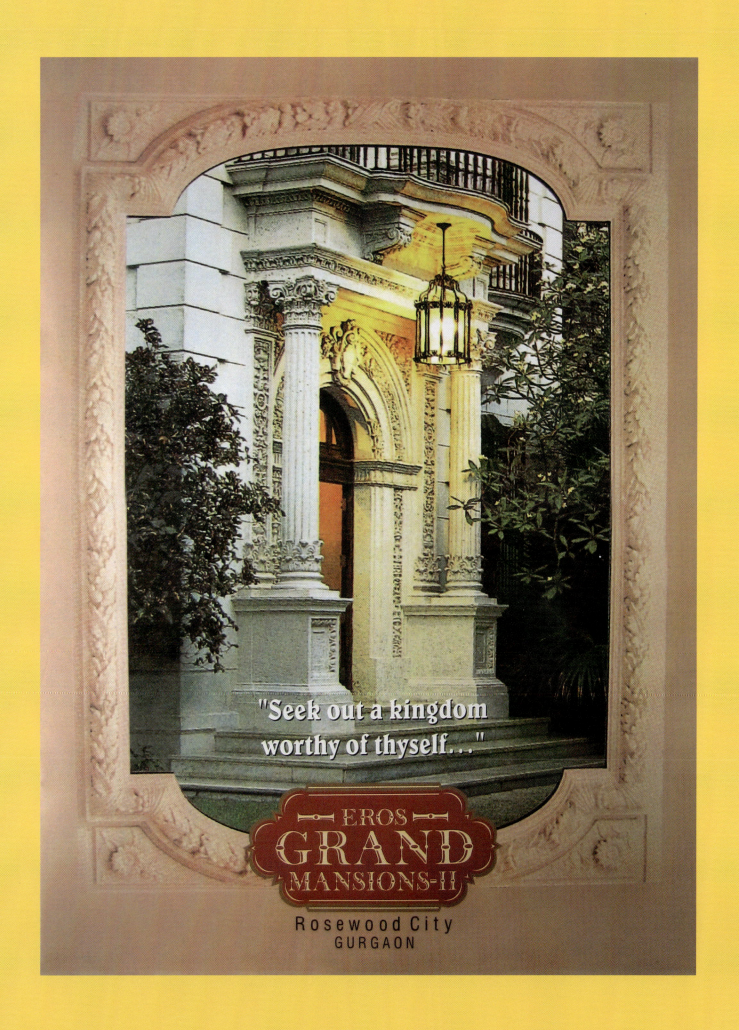

"Seek out a kingdom worthy of thyself…"

EROS
GRAND
MANSIONS-II

Rosewood City
GURGAON

Victoria Gardens in Delhi." An interesting take off on colonial history.... Omaxe, one of the big real-estate names in India, appropriates and interprets Ancient Egypt for one of its latest apartment townships, "Luxor" in Gurgaon. The advertisement claims that, where more than four hundred apartments are situated in nine towers,

> ...the World's greatest Civilization now comes alive in Gurgaon. Luxor Apartments and Penthouses. ... The place where Egyptian Grandeur mingles with ultra-modern lifestyle (and)...Egyptian architecture...hieroglyphs on walls, coloured sandstone, Egyptian paintings on the wall, and Luxor-inspired domes.[14]

Text and image reflect the production of transcultural connections, of a "world class" history, where the Indian/Hindu culture and Golden Age emerges as a parallel topography to that of Greek Antiquity, the Roman Empire, and the Egyptian Pharaohs. This is also manifest on the cover of an Eros brochure of Grand Mansions-II at Rosewood City, Gurgaon (figure 5). The slogan "Seek out a kingdom worthy of thyself", appeals to the potential buyer to internalize the advice that apparently Alexander the Great had been given by his father. The appeal is superimposed onto a baroque entrance of a huge house, however, not quite in tune with Alexander's period. In many ways, Europe serves as an index for historical weight and for the visualized distinction of those "who made it", be it Antiquity, Medieval Baroque, or Romantic landscape gardens, and late-19th-century suburban garden cities. "Europe" still counts as a luxury label with export quality. Maybe, one could argue, this is because for so many centuries several of its countries were associated with cultural superiority, successful and powerful imperial and colonial expansion, and international recognition.[15] Here, India is not alone in its visual and architectural mimesis: other countries that witnessed economic liberalization recently show a similar affinity, be it in China's Shanghai or Russia's Moscow.[16]

Why is Alexander appealing for the "modern maharajas"? We learn in the brochure that he was an "all conquering and free spirit", one of the "most prolific conquerors of all times", and he had even come to north India! Such a place is for those "forever seeking more out of life". The architecture represents "stately elegance and generous spaces...classical perfection and grand proportions...conquering the modern world of lifestyle yet once again...against constraints of space", the lack of which is so often a given in a megacity like Delhi. Again, we are reminded of Inden's statement of Bollywood's middle classes' Arcadia, when the Eros brochure claims to unveil a "saga of unparalleled lifestyle", for the "deserving few", the conquering and the power-hungry: "finally, couches can be placed far apart...you can give that big and exquisite Persian carpet its due place". Likewise, a guide to "good living" is wrapped up in the next quotation for the Grand Mansions project, where each villa has five bedrooms and imported bath fittings:

> Parthenon-like balconies, stately corridors, magnanimous reception areas with water bodies mingle easily with Jacuzzi, ensuite bathrooms, modular kitchen.... An ancient architecture conquers the modern age constraints of space and economy to broaden your world, while modern lifestyle and privileges make life amidst this glorious architecture a phenomenal experience.

What is meant by "Parthenon-like" can only be guessed, given the origin of the term in Ancient Greek temple architecture. The eclecticism imbued in this quote mirrors architect Gautam Bhatia's excellent portrayal of popular architectural styles and middle-class attitudes in north India, for which he coined the term "Punjabi Baroque". To Bhatia, this style represents a creative attempt to show and produce taste and distinction by appropriating elements from a vast range of other styles:

> Chandni Chowk Chippendale, Tamil Tiffany, Maratha Chauvinism, Bengali Asceticism, Akali Folly, Marwari Pragmatism, Punjabi Baroque, Bania Gothic, Bhaiyya Eclectic, Brahmin Medievalism, Parsi Propriety and Anglo-Indian Rococo, among others, are all part of the permanent collection of the streets, the new

urban galleries, the architectural canvas on public display.[17]

These visualized and spatialized mosaics are an attempt of the middle classes to avoid being classified as "provincial" and "uneducated", to display cultural competence in "world class" architecture.[18] By being familiar with one's own and world history, one qualifies as belonging to the knowing elite.

Themed and tamed nature

While exclusiveness is manifest in the advertisements for "world class" lifestyle by joining the global Indian with the nostalgia of a grand past, the "gated gaze" is also shaped by references to "nature" and paradisic "naturalness". In the ads, the culture-nature divide is blurred for a split second, when views of Arcadian landscape gardens are given, visually and metaphorically, suggesting a way of living where meadows are covered with morning dew; where silent sites for meditation and endless gazing are possible, in the presence of exotic domestic flora and fauna; where evenings are filled with peacock screams and laughter from the pool instead of car and truck noise or the sound of an airplane landing. This feeds into a growing desire among upwardly mobile urban middle classes for the acquisition and consumption of artificially created spaces for recreation from stressful work, in the form of themed zones, be they gated communities, fun parks, malls, or golf courses. The pleasure of enjoying nature and silence are often-mentioned attributes of a private enclave. These are positioned against the image of the "rest" of the city as inhuman, and often as "wild". Thus tamed and disciplined nature, and the affluence of "green" and lush gardens come to evoke the anxious idea of an "unnatural" outside that must be combated. Consider the following two advertisements: "*In a city full of concrete, a living garden resort to live and breathe. In Delhi. Victoria Gardens. Your Living Garden Resort*" (Victoria Gardens, Model Town) and "*Set amidst the fresh winds of an unpolluted atmosphere and landscaped gardens*" (Amrapali Village, Indirapuram). The more unplanned, ugly, dirty, and noisy the open city in the eyes of the upper and middle classes, the better sells the promise of a packaged honeymoon or gated Eden or Arcadia. Maybe this is why an advertisement

for a gated community entitled "AEZ Aloha" appears paradoxical only at second sight. The builders are promoting "super-luxury...apartments and penthouses, nestled in high-rise towers, inspired by the picturesque island of Hawaii...sun-kissed" and equipped with rare flora: "*Own a piece of this magical island and be a part of an elegant lifestyle.*" The idea of the remote island is visible only in the picture of a Goa-style beach with palm trees, a blue camping tent, and exotic flowers that remind one of Hula dancers. Interestingly, AEZ are also involved in a range of ways of "theme-ing" life and pleasure: their name stands behind fun parks like Carnival City, or theme malls like Gold Suk or Celebration Mall.

"Real" nature lies outside the fortress of the gated community, and indeed, different images of nature prevail and shape the everyday lives of the people living there, where meditation on a park bench is probably not even heard of. Partly farm land, partly deserted land, waiting to be fenced and turned into another colony, the contrast between themed and unrecognized nature could not be more drastic.

Exotic gender-bending in the living room

This article closes on a last anecdote from a shopping mall in Gurgaon, where a Feng Shui shop crowns the pleasures of consumption with the legitimization of objects equipped with spiritual power and traditional knowledge systems. In terms of lifestyle practice and commodification, hardly anything has attracted such a wide range of upper and lower middle-class citizens than Feng Shui and Vastu. They must be understood as strategies of dealing with modern life challenges such as competition at the workplace, infertility, exam stress, and familial tensions. But in their shadow, other lifestyle images and objects can be found, too. They are meant to hold wine-bottles, decorate shelves and walls. Their iconography displays a seemingly unconnected chain of "foreign", exotic, sexualized, and grotesque bodies: there are Afro-American jazz musicians and White cowboys, cricket-playing elephants and busts of Egyptian pharaohs. Yet, surprisingly many items depict women, either rural beauties out of a timeless Indian or South African village, or seductively dancing half-naked Europeans or porcelain figurines of shepherdesses in

6. Feng Shui aesthetics: Egyptian pharaohs and Black Beauty juxtaposed with trendy dolls at Kriti Creations, Khan Market, New Delhi, 2006. Photograph: R.S. Iyer.

French Rococo style, much like airport or tourist art, the equivalent to "Punjabi Baroque". One of the most surprising items I once saw in that shop was a glass table held by the figure of a naked black woman on her knees, bent forward, balancing the plate on her back. The shop owner told me that figures of African farmers and Egyptian pharaohs were a fairly new phenomenon and almost as popular as Feng Shui objects and Hindu deities. For him, they were a sign of India's exposure to globalization, a sign of modernity, and distinction (figures 6 and 7). Homi Bhabha[19] has written about the ambiguity of the racist stereotype, the exotic fetish, in which the Other surfaces as overwhelmingly sensual and absorbing and must at the same time be tamed by distancing him/her, either by means of classifying (as "dangerous") or by naturalizing (as "simple", "child-like"). In interesting ways, British colonialist stereotypes are appropriated in Indian contemporary middle-class aesthetics, shaping what could be termed as a neo-colonial paradigm. In this, however, Indian taste is in many ways echoing a global fascination with the picturesque, colonial, romantic, erotic, and oriental.

In conclusion, it could be argued that the iconography of the "enclaved gaze" reflects the

7. Impressions at Kriti Creations, Gurgaon, 2006. Photograph: Christiane Brosius.

aesthetic and aspirations of a new affluent and tentatively confident Indian middle class. The visual regime of this popular cosmopolitan imagination flaunts the notion that it is possible to distinguish oneself from others by putting on display and thus shaping a cosmopolitan lifestyle environment, or at least the idea of what it could be like. The pictures discussed are imbued with the desire to "belong to class", to be "world class", and for control over the allegedly unorderly, uncontrollable public. Yet, possibly the picture of the world as an enclave, despite the lures of glamour, power, and pleasure, is one within limiting and artificial boundaries, shaping, as Reddy has possibly rightly noted above, a "divide [with] a new edge".

NOTES

[1] C. Rammanohar Reddy, "A Tale of Two Indias", *Outlook*, January 10, 2005, p. 88.

[2] John Urry coined the term tourist gaze, a practice involving all senses, through which identities and world views are shaped discursively and performatively (*The Tourist Gaze: Leisure and Travel in Contemporary Societies*, London: Sage Publications, 1990).

[3] Leela Fernandes, "Nationalizing 'the Global': Media Images, Cultural Politics and the Middle Class in India", *Media, Culture & Society* 22(5), 2000, p. 612.

[4] Stuart Ewen, *All Consuming Images: The Politics of Style in Contemporary Culture*, New York: Basic Books, 1988, pp. 20, 58, 62.

[5] Ibid., p. 29; see also Anthony King, 2002. "Speaking from the Margins: 'Postmodernism', Transnationalism and the Imagining of Contemporary Indian Urbanity", in Richard Grant and J.R. Short (eds.), *Globalization and the Margins*, New York: Palgrave Macmillan, pp. 72–90.

[6] Ronald Inden, "Transnational Class, Erotic Arcadia and Commercial Utopia in Hindi Films", in Christiane Brosius and Melissa Butcher (eds.), *Image Journeys. Audio-Visual Media and Cultural Change in India*, New Delhi: Sage Publications, 1999, p. 48.

[7] Ibid., p. 59.

[8] Marc Augé, *Non-Places: Introduction to an Anthropology of Supermodernity*, London and New York: Verso, 1995.

[9] Evan Mckenzie, "The Dynamics of Privatopia: Private Residential Governance in the USA", in Georg Glasze, Chris Webster, and Klaus Frantz (eds.), *Private Cities: Global and Local Perspectives*, London and New York: Routledge, 2006, p. 9.

[10] Construction for this township is still ongoing. See http://www.vatikagroup.com/Residential/VatikaCityGurgaon/home.html (accessed on August 4, 2007).

[11] Teresa Caldeira, "Fortified enclaves. The New Urban Segregation", in Jan Lin and Christopher Mele, *The Urban Sociology Reader*, London and New York: Routledge, 2005, pp. 328–29.

[12] Walter Benjamin, "Paris, Capital of the Nineteenth Century", in *The Arcades Project*, Cambridge, Mass. and London: Harvard University Press, 1999, p. 23.

[13] Ibid., p. 17.

[14] *TOI Online*, Rohit Karir: "Live Life Egyptian-Size".

[15] Veronique Dupont, "The Idea of a New Chic Delhi through Publicity Hype", in Romi Khosla (ed.), *The Idea of Delhi*, Mumbai: Marg Publications, 2005, pp. 78–93.

[16] Glasze et al., *Private Cities*, cited in note 9.

[17] Gautam Bhatia, *Punjabi Baroque, and other Memories of Architecture*, Delhi: Penguin, 1994, p. 32.

[18] See also Krishna Menon, "Inventive Mimesis in New Delhi: The Temples of Chhattarpur", in Wim Denslagen and Niels Gutschow (eds.), *Architectural Imitations: Reproductions and Pastiches in East and West*, Maastricht: Shaker Publishing, 2005, pp. 98–123.

[19] Homi Bhabha, *The Location of Culture*, London and New York: Routledge, 1997 (1st edition 1994).

ADDITIONAL REFERENCES

Daniel Miller, Peter Jackson, Nigel Thrift, Beverly Holbrook, and Michael Rowlands, *Shopping, Place and Identity*, London and New York: Routledge, 1998.

Mica Nava, "Cosmopolitan Modernity: Everyday Imaginaries and the Registers of Difference", *Theory, Culture & Society* 19(1-2), 2002, pp. 81–99.

INDEX

Page numbers in bold indicate
captions

CONTRIBUTORS

Jyotindra Jain, formerly Director of the Crafts Museum, New Delhi, is Professor at the School of Arts & Aesthetics, Jawaharlal Nehru University, New Delhi. A former Alexander-von-Humboldt Fellow, Homi Bhabha Fellow, Visiting Professor at Harvard University at the Centre for the Study of World Religions, and recipient of the 1998 Prince Claus Award, his publications include: *Ganga Devi: Tradition and Expression in Mithila Painting*; *Other Masters: Five Contemporary Folk and Tribal Artists of India*; *Kalighat Painting: Images from a Changing World*; and *Indian Popular Culture: "The Conquest of the World as Picture"*. He edited the Marg volume *Picture Showmen: Insights into the Narrative Tradition in Indian Art* (1998). As Director of *CIVIC: Centre for Indian Visual Culture* he is engaged in creating a vast digital archive of Indian popular visual culture.

Sumathi Ramaswamy is Professor of History at Duke University, Durham, North Carolina. She is the author of *Passions of the Tongue: Language Devotion in Tamil India, 1891–1970* (1997) and *The Lost Land of Lemuria: Fabulous Geographies, Catastrophic Histories* (2004). She has also edited a volume entitled *Beyond Appearances? Visual Practices and Ideologies in Modern India* (2003), and has recently completed a book manuscript entitled *The Goddess and the Nation: Picturing Mother India.*

Christopher Pinney is Visiting Crowe Professor of Art History at Northwestern University, Evanston, Illinois and Professor of Anthropology and Visual Culture at University College London. He has held visiting positions at the Australian National University, the University of Chicago, the University of Cape Town, and Jawaharlal Nehru University, New Delhi. His publications include *Camera Indica: The Social Life of Indian Photographs* (1997) and *"Photos of the Gods": The Printed Image and Political Struggle in India* (2004). The text of the Panizzi Lectures he delivered at the British Library in 2006 is forthcoming in early 2008.

Anuradha Kapur has written widely on the theatre, including a book *Actors, Pilgrims, Kings and Gods: the Ramlila at Ramnagar* (1993, 2004). She has taught and directed in India and abroad and her theatre work has had occasion to travel extensively in India and to several festivals abroad. She is presently Director of the National School of Drama, New Delhi.

Yousuf Saeed, a Delhi-based independent filmmaker and researcher, has been making documentary films for the last 16 years. His short films such as *Basant, Inside Ladakh*, and *The Train to Heaven* have been shown at various Indian and international film festivals, academic venues, and on TV channels. His most recent work is a feature-length documentary on the classical music traditions in Pakistan. Yousuf has also been collecting popular printed images and calendar art of Indian Muslims for the last 12 years. In 2004, he was awarded the Sarai Fellowship to work on the syncretic symbolism of Muslim poster art, which culminated in a research paper as well a larger collection of images.

Ranjani Mazumdar is an independent filmmaker and Associate Professor of Cinema Studies at the School of Arts & Aesthetics at Jawaharlal Nehru University, New Delhi. Her publications and films focus on urban cultures, popular cinema, gender, and the cinematic city. She is the author of *Bombay Cinema: An Archive of the City*, and is currently co-authoring a book on the Indian film industry for the British Film Institute. Her documentaries include *Delhi Diary 2001* on memory and violence in the city of Delhi and *The Power of the Image* (co-directed) – a television series on Bombay cinema.

Savia Viegas holds a Ph.D. in Art History and has taught at K.C. College, University of Mumbai. A former Senior Fulbright and Ministry of Culture (India) Fellow, her other interests include photography, museums, and oral traditions. She has founded and heads Saxtti, a rural NGO in Goa. Saxtti works with children and village communities, endeavouring to empower them to be at the centre of development. Savia is presently completing a book on the social history of Goan family photographs.

Christiane Brosius is Assistant Professor at the Department of Social Anthropology, South Asia Institute of the University of Heidelberg in Germany. With a background in art history and art education (photography, printmaking, and drawing), she has researched and published widely on Hindu nationalist media politics (*Empowering Visions*, 2005), about "ritual agency", urban anthropology, diaspora studies, and commercial Hindi film. She is currently working on a book about cosmopolitanism of the emergent middle classes in India and overseas. Brosius is founding member of *Tasveer Ghar* (House of Pictures) – A Digital Network of South Asian Popular Visual Culture (www. tasveerghar.net).